THE THIRD PERSON IN THE ROOM

Stories of Relationships at a Turning Point

Bea V. Larsen, Esq.

Nolan Kerr Press

CINCINNATI, OHIO

Bea V. Larsen, Esq./Nolan Kerr Press
1325 Lance Ct.
Lebanon, OH 45036
www.nolankerr.com

Publisher's Note: This is a work of nonfiction. Names, characters, places, and incidents are a product of the author's imagination. Locales and public names are sometimes used for atmospheric purposes. Any resemblance to actual people, living or dead, or to businesses, companies, events, institutions, or locales is completely coincidental.

Nolan Kerr Press© 2019
Cover design by Max Nolan
Cover photo by Paula Norton

The Third Person in the Room: Stories of Relationships at a Turning Pont
Nolan Kerr Press
ISBN 978-1-7333402-0-5

Contact Bea Larsen at: beavlarsen@gmail.com
Contact Nolan Kerr Press at: info@nolankerr.com

To my former clients who, at their most vulnerable moments, trusted me with their fears and dreams

What people are saying about

The Third Person in the Room

"A winner for the inquisitive. It teaches, you learn, and enjoy."
— Hon. Jack Sherman, U.S. Magistrate Judge for the Southern District of Ohio (1989- 2003)

"I learned more about communicating and relationships from reading Bea's essays than I have in 43 years as an attorney. There are a number of situations that I will now approach differently than I have in the past. "
— John Norwine, Executive Director, Cincinnati Bar Association (1995-2016)

"Bea Larsen does not consider this to be a how-to book, though it is one. This book is complex, non-prescriptive, and offers no promises. What it does offer is a lifetime's worth of professional and personal observations about relationships of all kinds, delivered with great intelligence and perception. And heart. I intend to give copies to all my coupled and uncoupled friends whether they are at 'turning points' or not."
— Howard Wells, Consulting Editor

"Readers of Bea Larsen's stories from her life and long professional career will benefit from the wisdom and calm assurance she has offered those who have met with her for help with their relationships. I imagine sitting on the long couch in her office, gleaning the insights she has gained and the lessons she has taught herself about handling one's own relationships, and moving on as we age."
— Karen Faaborg, Professor Emerita, University of Cincinnati

"There is a selective, easy stroll to compassion. And there is a 'where the rubber of difficult human circumstances and interactions meets the road of life's obstacles and trying times' trek. With grace and wisdom, Bea Larsen guides us along the tough road to compassion, and we end our journey wiser and more thoughtful. After reading her book, you will thank her for her honesty, her humanness, her courage, and her guidance to become our best selves."

– Christine A. Lottman Professor Emerita, University of Cincinnati School of Social Work

"Readers of author Bea Larsen's narratives will find a storehouse of personal and professional wisdom, enriched by her skillful gift of language, refined over decades, to give expression, without judgment, to a number of life's mysteries that challenge individuals to cope. The calm yet penetrating observations of complexities in relationships are a balm to those struggling through periods of crisis. That makes *The Third Person in the Room* a must read."

– Hon. Nathaniel R. Jones, Judge, United States Court of Appeals for the Sixth Circuit (1979-2002), Blank Rome LLC

"Bea Larsen has written an elegant book of insightful short essays which offer wisdom for the taking. Reading her concise personal and professional reflections is a welcome journey through the possibility of learning and growth during times of challenge. She articulates the potential of the well-timed question, spoken without judgment or disdain, for helping someone explore another avenue, headed toward new insight in a relationship. Bea's book is an intelligent, straightforward reference for life at home and in the office. I highly recommend treating yourself to this engaging series of meaningful stories."

– Susan Jasbeck Steinberg, PhD, Clinical Psychologist

"After 40 years as a professional mediator, by reading *Third Person in the Room*, I enrolled as Bea Larsen's student in a Master Level

Graduate Program in life. Bea became my Professor, Mentor, and Model for personal as well as professional growth. Like *Tuesdays with Morrie*, this book provides life lessons borne of Bea's wide personal experience. Much more than a self-help primer, *Third Person* is a tool box for resolving conflict in our own lives as well as a fountain of ideas for helping professionals help individuals, families and organizations. Not being able to put the book down, I laughed with and marveled at Bea's wisdom delivered with reflection and humility. Reading this book is a close second to having a long glass of wine with Bea in her Cincinnati living room."

– Forrest ("Woody") Mosten, Mediator, Author and Collaborative Lawyer, San Diego and Beverly Hills, CA

"We join this gracious and wise woman "in the room' as she imparts her sage musings about relationships. Her insights are poetic and profound, nudging us to examine how we connect with others. This book can be devoured in one sitting or enjoyed and savored in small doses. Like fine wine, it is seasoned, impeccable, and refreshing."

– Charlene Ventura, President and CEO, YWCA of Greater Cincinnati (1988 – 2015)

"Supplementing her career-acquired insights is Larsen's experience of a fifty year marriage that involved the raising of three children. Here, too, she provides a revealing, personal account of struggles with boundaries, secrets, and all manner of communicative pitfalls."

– Robert Shulman, M.D., Psychiatrist

"Anyone who has encountered conflict in relationships – and that encompasses everyone – will find this compendium of thoughtful reflections by a seasoned family lawyer and mediator a stimulating source of intellectual nourishment. Larsen goes well beyond the confines of self-help advice and into the realm of deeper introspection and questioning. She provides guidance tempered by the wisdom of knowing there are no easy answers to life's many questions."

— *Sherry Davis, Attorney, Mediator*

CONTENTS

FOREWORD

Dear Reader,

Welcome to what might be the most helpful guide to navigating relationships under stress you will read this year...or maybe ever.

Bea Larsen did not intend to write a self-help book, and still denies that she has. *The Third Person in the Room* is a collection of stories of mostly well-intended people struggling within themselves and with each other through difficult times, stories framed more as inquiries than advice. The author is as much a student asking questions as a teacher offering answers; she draws advice from journalists and playwrights, psychologists and anthropologists, neurologists and politicians, and weaves their insights into explanations for how our best intentions can sometimes go wrong. In these stories her marriage, law office, and mediation conference room become laboratories for learning.

Of course, these inquiries are posed through her own unique lens. Bea was born to Jewish Russian immigrant parents who settled in New York and thought FDR was a hero. She studied at Antioch College in Yellow Springs, Ohio, where she met and married a reserved Scandinavian Midwesterner from a Lutheran family that believed FDR was the devil incarnate. They raised three children in the turbulent 1960s before she entered law school as one of only two women in her class. She co-founded a public defender office at the age of 43, ran for judge as the only woman at 50, started a private law practice at 51, and became a mediator at 57. She was an early founder of what became an international collaborative law movement in the mid-1990s, and an activist for political civility well into her 80s. From all this comes a woman with traditional roots, a progressive bent, and no small amount of ambition, who managed to forge an insatiable curiosity with unshakable kindness and an empiricist's insistence on evidence, to produce the truly useful observations of the human condition we find in each of these stories.

The first thing you are likely to notice, and appreciate, about this book is that Bea Larsen does not waste words. Poignant two-page stories of everyday people's experiences are brought forth not as platitudes or self-expositions, but as humble lessons and insights—theirs and hers, drawn clearly and concisely. She has done the work of finding the kernels of truth for us, and serves them up plainly and elegantly for us to see.

Brevity is not the only way this author respects her subjects and readers alike. Refreshingly clear and honest discussion of common but often concealed concerns about such topics as sex, shame, fear, mental illness, intimacy, and money assumes both our intelligence and our maturity. While she frankly acknowledges her own weaknesses and missteps as friend and professional, the human foibles of others are almost universally accepted within Bea's whole-some worldview. There is no hint of superiority in her assessments of the mistakes of clients whose marriages are ending, only compassion and understanding. We all can be received in Bea's Graceland where average people's all-too-human stories of fear and love, worry and celebration, breakdown and breakthrough resonate with critical moments in our own lives; for here they are examined through an empathic lens that lets us see and learn and hope to do better ourselves.

You might find yourself wondering, as I often have, whether Bea's wisdom is the product of nature or nurture. Was this author born compassionately insightful, shrewd and generous, both critical and open minded...or did her life experiences shape her to be so? In the Introduction, she seems to give much of the credit to her loving parents, but I wonder. Maybe she was shaped by her parents' kindness, but we only know them through her eyes. Having watched her navigate her own challenges, big and small, I confess my awe of her gentle, confident embrace of life, and I wonder if, even suspect that, it was she who found much of that goodness in her parents, as she does in her clients, friends, and family.

Perhaps it is her interest in people and their motivations, honed by the developed instincts of a mediator, that makes her the studied observer of how formative experiences and social pressures lead people toward or away from healthy choices that we learn about in this book. It's these observations that imbue every essay with life lessons, set in familiar contexts, that travel well; that give advice by example rather than lecture; and that encourage us to look at our shadows with understanding and love. There are no bad guys in these stories of missed moments, failed relationships, anger, and betrayal. There are only weaknesses or flaws that most of us can recognize in ourselves and in others we love.

How does she do that? Many writers offer advice from their experience, but Bea does not give advice. She lets her subjects' experiences do the talking, contributing her own focus while often weaving in relevant insights from experts. That all of this is contained in brief, remarkably readable essays, sets this work apart.

You might also notice what seem at first like contradictions, or paradoxes, but which I have come to associate with wisdom. For example, how can one person be accomplished enough to receive every professional honor and award her profession has to offer – which she has – and be humble enough to still be studying the latest publications on her craft – which she does, while constantly re-examining the adequacy of her personal and professional efforts, as she also does in so many of these stories? How does one objectively and pragmatically analyze human foibles and shortcomings without being critical? How can someone who worked to honor and preserve her own marriage of fifty-three years be so understanding of those whose marriages are coming apart, sometimes through their own failings?

I don't know the source of Bea Larsen's wisdom, but I can speak to its authenticity.

I met Bea in the late 1970s when I was directing a criminal justice planning agency, with grants to offer worthy organizations, and she was directing a public defender office in need of funds. Her reputation preceded her request, as she and her office were recognized throughout the community for diligence and effectiveness. Perhaps they were too effective, as it turned out; vigorous defense of "criminals" has never been uniformly appreciated. Prosecutors and police must work harder for convictions and courts contend with more and longer trials, all adding stresses and cost to a jaded system that, truth be known, often views criminally charged defendants as guilty until proven innocent. Bea's struggle to save her office was noble but futile; what it was not was rancorous and ugly. The loss to Bea and her idealistic warriors for the marginalized was deeply felt, but without evident bitterness. The fix was in. She knew it, fought it, lost, and accepted the defeat like a seasoned sports coach after a tough loss.

Not long thereafter, at the urging of friends, she ran in a county-wide election for judge. With no name recognition, she and her passionate volunteers knocked on doors, gave speeches at churches and picnics...and lost. Undiminished, she accepted the outcome with characteristic sincerity and grace.

Is such dignity learned or innate? Does it result from the acceptance of what is, or enable it? "Don't howl at the moon," she's fond of saying. Wise acceptance is more than resignation to one's fate; it doesn't give up or give in, it sees and accepts what's true. It does not waste time and energy fighting with reality, it looks beyond impasse to purpose and improvement.

In short order, Bea was recruited into the leadership ladder of the Cincinnati Bar Association, eventually becoming the CBA's first woman president.

As community recognition and awards piled up, she grew even more humble, once telling me awards should not be taken too seriously as members of professional organizations like giving them to each other to boost their resumes. Maybe, but some awards are only given rarely and only to people whose contributions to others have been widely recognized as meaningful and extraordinary; Bea has received all of those, too.

You can read details of her biography in the Introduction. What might not be evident there is the steady, calm strength she brings to every person and every problem she meets. She feels deeply without being emotional, she sees and meets people and problems where they are with clear eyes, keen intelligence, and a heartfelt purpose to help. This has made her an excellent and sought after mediator, mentor, and confidante to many, and a close, valued friend. That loving is now yours, should you choose to accept it, in this book.

–Robert Rack, Chief Circuit Mediator, U.S. Court of Appeals for the Sixth Circuit, 1981-2010.

Robert Rack was an early founder of court-based mediation in the U.S., starting a mediation office in the U.S. Court of Appeals for the Sixth Circuit in Cincinnati in 1981. From there he consulted in the formation of mediation programs in courts throughout the United States, and in Asia and the Middle East. He retired from the Court in 2010 and co-founded Beyond Civility with Bea Larsen to engage civic and political leaders in programs designed to facilitate cross-partisan understanding and communication for effective democratic governance. Follow his blog at www.ontheotherhand.xyz.

INTRODUCTION

I treasure those moments when a friend brings me a personal concern, and their worried look eases as we talk. Sharing my experience and the knowledge gleaned over eight decades---as an attorney for fifty years, a mediator for twenty-five of those years, and a wife and mother since my early twenties---allows me to offer an intimate view of relationships gone awry, some repaired, others ended. This book is a collection of short essays that frame and define that experience, many stories drawn from my professional life, others quite personal.

Picture this: I'm sitting in my office, a space made cozy and warm by design. I am relaxed and breathe easy. A husband and wife face me seated on opposite ends of my long couch. No table or desk stands between us as a buffer to the intimacy that will soon develop among the three of us. They are tense. They hold my gaze but do not look at each other. Sometimes angry, always sad, they have come to find a way forward that protects their children and offers mutual respect, even kindness.

So it begins, the relationship between a divorce mediator and two people who no longer see themselves as a couple, their connection stretched to the breaking point in the months, or possibly years, of disappointment and conflict that now dominates their lives. They do not seek a way to come together again, to reconcile, but rather a path to go forward alone.

As they tell me their stories, some in a halting voice, others with urgency, I enter their lives as the third person in the room, both an observer and a guide, to help them turn chaos into order. Together we build their separate hopes for the future into a mutually acceptable plan.

For more than twenty-five years, I have written about the relationship dynamics of divorcing couples who chose to mediate their differences and retain control over the decisions that will frame their and their children's futures instead of yielding to the litigation process and judicial court orders. I seek to draw from their stories the wisdom gained, the lessons learned, both from their missteps and from their developing insights.

As I do so, events or patterns from my own past often come to mind and become part of the truths that emerge. Their intimate disclosures, my observation of their back-and-forth talk, the looks of disdain or compassion, all evoke personal memories, some from many years ago. Looking back, I see the person I used to be in the many rooms in which I grew up, married, raised a family, developed a legal career, experienced joys and suffered losses. Remembering those years, now from a distance, I am the third person in the rooms of my past as well.

My former mediation clients appear in many of my essays, so it might be assumed that I am addressing only readers whose relationships either are on the verge of breakup or have already collapsed. Not so. Although guidance may be found in these pages for those who are preparing to walk away from their partner, glimpses of my client's lives, or of my own, present a microcosm of every relationship. Those couples who decide to part ways offer a vivid picture of what others who consider themselves to be on safe ground may on occasion be experiencing, even if only for fleeting moments of any one day. For anyone in a loving relationship is (or will be tomorrow) feeling some measure of disequilibrium. Even those who are secure may sometimes be bored or wish for greater intimacy, or more independence. Their secure connection may not be at risk, just uneasy from time to time, and needing attention.

Because my clients have already given up, the reader can enter their private world and observe their crisis, a vantage point otherwise available only when close friends or family members bring us their miseries. But when we are drawn into the lives of those we know well and with whom we have a strong bond, our view is one-sided. We are not dispassionate observers, for we have an active role to play, perhaps to be a loyal friend or a supportive parent.

When marriage partners in mediation talked about what was driving them apart, I sometimes asked about their parents' marriages. I noted the differences in how they each described their early family lives and thought they often made the disappointments now taking center stage understandable. No doubt when we are young, without conscious thought, we develop future expectations from our unique family culture that we later project onto those we choose as partners. For years these expectations may remain unspoken, even unacknowledged, until discontent arises.

As my essays often include glimpses of the ever-evolving relationship with my husband, Len, particularly as we sought to communicate when tension was in the air, understanding the differences in our formative years and the emotional climate of our childhood homes may add to a deeper understanding of the stories told, the insights recounted.

One of my earliest memories, as a child of five or six, is standing next to my mother and father as they stood hugging each other---and I attempt to pry them apart so I could enter and be part of the embrace. Today I can still picture them sitting companionably close, seriously talking things over. When family members or friends had problems they rarely hid them from view but discussed them without restraint. Emotional disclosure was intrinsic to my family culture.

Len, of Norwegian descent, once told me this joke: "Did you hear the one about the Norwegian farmer who loved his wife so much, he almost told her?" That bespeaks volumes about the myth of the silent Norwegian male, and the reality of the home in which Len grew up. Over the many years when I came to know and love his parents, I never saw them fondly embrace or express emotion, except perhaps frustration about some day-to-day common mishap. Yet I never doubted their loyalty or love for each other.

In the early years of our marriage, Len's reluctance to talk about his feelings, even as I probed, was troubling. He was a quiet man who often hid his feelings, sometimes even from himself, almost always from others. Reading his silence as rejection, I would withdraw, only to be drawn back by a tentative loving touch. Slowly, over the years, we developed the skill and knowledge to honor our differences and eventually to communicate with greater ease.

This is not a how-to-book in which I share the wisdom of my long experience by prescribing a specific better path for you to follow.

Instead, I tell stories which may bring to life your personal remembrances or experiences, or that evoke thoughtfulness without the resistance engendered by judgment. You are free to decide if a story fits who you are at this moment, if it makes sense or not. Or perhaps on occasion you will be motivated to share the thoughts that a story evokes with an intimate friend or partner, casually, as if to say: *Here's an interesting idea.* You're offering a story about someone else, not a prescription for how your other should change, which might be met with resistance, not thoughtful consideration. Who knows where the sharing of a thoughtful insight can lead?

Just as fiction and drama allow us to project ourselves into the lives of others, to try on another persona, the sharing of the experience of strangers while we are off stage and safe leaves us free to draw from their lives whatever we wish, with no demands, no lectures. You may also find warnings, new ideas, or even inspiration to change your own life in some way.

Perhaps this is all you need to know to now dip into the essays being presented here. Yet as an author unknown to most of you who have read this far, I am asking you to trust in the wisdom I've gleaned over many years. If I were asked to put my trust in someone new to me, I'd like to know more about them, so more is provided in *A Personal History*, which can be found at the end of this book.

CHAPTER ONE

COMMUNICATION

Suffer the Silence

How readily we blame others when our conversational styles don't match. I used to be a master at it.

Normally my thoughts translate into speech with virtually no time delay. But when I talked with my husband, especially when I was saying something I thought important, I was frequently met with silence. Within only a nanosecond, I would be wondering about the reason for his lack of an immediate response. Was it anger, or boredom, or even worse, disdain? And in the instant it took me to speculate about his possible motives, I would notice what seemed a purposeful lack of eye contact as well. So---need I even say it---I faulted him for this communication impasse. Early in life, I learned by observing my mother to respond to rejection (for this was how it felt) by receding into silence. But my husband had also learned well how to protect himself at such times. So in response to my pointed withdrawal, he might studiously refocus on something he was reading, or quickly react to a welcomed interruption---the phone, a child, birds on the feeder.

And all of this avoidance, our disconnect, could be complete in less than a minute.

It took me about twenty-five of my married years, and professional help, to figure a way out of this communication quandary.

The symptom that drew us into counseling was my insomnia (and a twitching eyelid) when Len began taking our young grandchildren flying with him in the small plane he piloted. My speculations ran wild as I vividly pictured emergencies that could befall them high in the sky. My attempts to talk about this failed miserably. Here is what I learned: Some people, and clearly Len was one, seek more time than others to process their thoughts before committing them to speech. Perhaps someday scientists will identify the neural connections that govern such differences, but for whatever reason---whether it is innate, cultural or due to parental modeling---it's important for us to recognize and honor the reality that there are many different communication styles. The blameworthy motivations I had long been assigning made no sense.

With this new understanding, I would carefully choose my times for significant conversations, when there were no obvious distractions and we could talk for a while. When I started an exchange of importance to me, after speaking, I simply remained quiet. I did not ask rapid follow up questions in pursuit of an immediate reply. Nor did I pout. Several moments might pass, sometimes even an intervening comment made (by him) about something appearing on the landscape. But, I still waited.

A meaningful answer always came.

I eventually learned the lesson well: suffer the silence.

(Note: Len agreed to take a pilot friend along when flying with the grandchildren.)

Sponging

He said: "So, I hear you got the promotion. Another woman sleeps her way to the top."

She was silent at first. Although unnerved by this sarcastic taunt, she took a moment to consider her response.

Then she said: "You think that's what folks in the office believe? Can you help me track that rumor down?"

Surprisingly, her reaction exhibited not even a hint of defensiveness. That's because she was sponging, a technique I learned some years ago from Deborah Pearce, a teacher, coach, and master of the art of communication.

The concept of sponging is so valuable, I've posted it on my blog, and eagerly describe it to colleagues, friends, mediation clients and anyone else who will listen. It's a way of responding when you are verbally attacked that turns a conversation in a positive direction instead of allowing it to spiral into negativity.

This approach calls for mindful redirection. When confronted with a hostile remark, an insult, or even veiled sarcasm, avoid an immediate response. Instead, consciously absorb the belief of the speaker---soak it up like a sponge. Frame your answer from that vantage point, and watch the wind empty from your rival's sails.

Some examples:

1. A divorced mother to her former spouse: "When the kids leave your house for school, they look like they got dressed in the dark or slept in their clothes."

The father's likely automatic response: "I haven't noticed them looking so great when they come over here from your place."

But the father's response when sponging: "It's a problem. By the time they get to breakfast, it's too late to make them change. How do you handle it?"

2. A divorce lawyer represents a husband who is anticipating a sharp decline in income. He conveys this information to the wife's lawyer.

The wife's lawyer's likely automatic response: "Give me a break. That's what they all say."

But when sponging, the wife's lawyer says: "Of course, he's anxious about paying support. Who wouldn't be? Show me how he has documented his income projections."

3. Wife to husband taking part in mediation: "For years, you never had time for the kids. Now you're Mr. Mom."

The husband's likely automatic reply: "When's the last time you actually cooked them a meal?"

But when sponging, he says: "You're right. I relied on you more than I had any right to. I'm going to need your help learning the ropes with the kids."

For most of us, reacting self-protectively, even aggressively, is still our first line of defense. But caustic remarks raise the temperature of any discussion and once we respond defensively, antagonism escalates and little gets accomplished. Conflict needs to be diffused, not escalated. It takes practice. When our emotions are stirred, we need to take a critical pause before responding, to bring the technique to mind.

A disgruntled mediation client recently called to suggest that he was wasting his time and money in our sessions, as we had reached few agreements. My initial reaction was to resent being devalued, and I wanted to point out his negative contributions had slowed the process down. But after a pause, I sponged. I acknowledged his frustration and the difficult emotional climate of these delicate discussions. Then I asked for his suggestions for making progress. We had a good talk. He expressed gratitude and a commitment to continue.

All three examples above gave rise to a useful, calm discussion. Skilled negotiators work to set a positive emotional tone, but discord often seeps into even the best-planned conversations. Having a few well-practiced techniques on hand to call upon when an important

conversation is on a downward slide can save the day. Sponging--
pausing, then acknowledging (not agreeing with) the perspective of
the other and asking for help addressing the problem---can return a
conversation to solid ground.

So the next time, if the goal is understanding and a positive outcome, pause, and visualize a sponge.

"We Just Can't Talk"

"We just can't talk": the sad refrain of so many disappointed partners and likely of others still struggling to ward off failure. Surely they talked early on, when they were first getting acquainted. But as greater familiarity grows, and as minor and perhaps significant disappointments accumulate, some opt for saying nothing. Perhaps they are unable to find just the right words. Perhaps they yearn to be authentic but fear further distance or hurt. Others talk nonstop but in accusatory mode, desperate for acknowledgment but succeeding only in driving a partner further away. Oddly, many partners report that once they have made the decision to part, and tension recedes due to that resolve, ease of communication returns, but sadly only after all passion has flown. Is there something to be learned here?

Some who are struggling to overcome the silences often receive advice to try active listening, a technique in which they determine to not interrupt when each other is talking, then feed back what they have just heard, as a way of regenerating communication. On an intellectual level, these techniques have always made good sense to me, even though my own success in using them was abysmal. My mediation clients often report that their partner's feedback was tinged with sarcasm or boredom. The resentments are too firmly established for it to work. So, my interest was aroused when, some years ago, I read about the research of Dr. John Gottman, a psychologist at the University of Washington. He studied 130 newly married couples over a six-year period, tracking how they handled disagreement. Many reported they tried active listening and feedback techniques.

Dr. Gottman then compared these couples to an older study that followed successful marriages for thirteen years. He found that people who stayed together almost never used such listening techniques. What the marriages that seemed to work did have in common, according to Gottman, was that the husband was willing to be influenced by his wife. The good doctor said, "We found that only those newly-wed men who are accepting of influence from their wives are winding up in happy stable marriages." Now, I am not so naive as to believe for one moment that this is all it takes, but I clipped this article, gave it to my husband, and sent a copy to my daughter and, of course, to my sons.

The Second Question

I talk to people in elevators. Even unfamiliar faces open to a smile with a passing comment on the weather and a "How are you?" Almost invariably the answer is "Fine." And in moments we part, wishing each other well. A graceful verbal *pas de deux*.

But this story can take unexpected turns.

Seated in a restaurant some months ago, a woman approached me. She was familiar but out of our usual context. Then in but a second, I recognized her, a physician I used to see annually, until she left her private practice for an administrative position.

My smile met hers, and she asked, "How are you?"

"Fine," I said.

Then she asked, "Really fine?"

It was no longer an elevator conversation. Not settling for the usual dance, she had moved beyond the pro forma query and the automatic response.

As it happened, I was in good spirits, so I reaffirmed my initial answer. But later I recalled her second question and was grateful for her persistent interest. It caused me to consider how often I asked only the first question, even of close friends and family. Was I too busy, or too self-absorbed to ask, or maybe I'd rather not know?

Why would I rather not know?

On giving it serious thought, I recognized that between youth and my middle years, my behavior had shifted. When our kids were still young and became ill, I snapped into action, taking responsibility for their recovery with a purposeful ease. I had the power and control to select the right doctor and administer the care that would make them well. This was the role a parent should play and I did. By taking charge, my anxiety eased.

But years later, when our children were grown and independent, a major medical issue arose for our adult son. This time my husband,

Len, became the more attentive parent. When surgery was scheduled, he traveled some distance to join his wife by his side. Afterward it was Len who frequently called to ask how the recovery and follow up treatment were going. I waited to be told and was to some degree avoidant. No less concerned, but having ceded the important decisions to others, I backed away---and my anxiety grew.

I think this is why. When one of our adult kids faced a problem, Len could listen and be empathic without believing he had to influence or direct the outcome. Not me---I slipped back to my old script, longing to protect even grown children and help them reestablish their equilibrium. But now I no longer had the ability to do so. I had to acknowledge a new boundary, but since I was no longer in charge, worry took over. My withdrawal at the time of crisis was an attempt, albeit a failed one, to be self-protective.

It has taken me far too long to learn that sometimes simply listening, seeking to understand, and expressing sympathy are enough. I do not need to offer the right advice and take responsibility for a decision being made. Giving up that mandate, which still requires a mindful pause, restores calm.

Once again a personal insight informed my professional practice. When I meet a client to discuss their concern, my first question is often, "How are you doing?" And if the response is perfunctory, I ask the second question.

Now, with friends and family, sometimes I ask the third question, "Is there anything I can do?"

I expect their answer will probably be no, but the question is an invitation to talk further if and when the time is right, to have a conversation that may serve us well and enrich an intimate connection.

Just the asking brings comfort, for both of us. And on these new terms, I really do want to know.

Speaking of Love

I enter a room, interrupting a phone conversation, which soon ends with the words *I love you.*

These three words have become a ubiquitous sign-off, often spoken to a child but also to a spouse or partner. A generational divide must be at work, for I rarely heard such farewells (except possibly when whispered) in my youth or even in my middle years.

They leave me feeling somewhat disquieted, the same unease I experience with every passing. *Have a good day.*

Inwardly, I chastise myself for my cynicism and even wonder at my own awkwardness when a dear friend expects these parting words from me. I usually smile but remain silent.

I was married for many years to a man who rarely said those words. But he did write them from time to time, on letters and cards that came with the anniversary flowers, and admittedly I saved them. But not being told by my husband that he loved me rarely gave me much pause, for we both conveyed love in so many wordless ways. The absence of the spoken phrase was not of much import.

But today, as a sensitive relationship topic, it is pervasive. Witness the number of television sit-coms that deal with a male character's apparent inability, or great difficulty, in putting those three words together in consecutive order when talking with a loved one face to face.

Some years ago, the stellar actor and playwright, Wallace Shawn remarked, "The difficulty of saying 'I love you' is that it presupposes that you know who 'I' is and that you know who 'you' is." A thought-provoking comment.

Suppose you say the words *I love you* and just hours later you find yourself greatly annoyed because once again your spouse has failed to meet you on time. Suppose moments after you speak the words to a child, he makes a disrespectful remark and you display what seems like irrational anger? Can it all make you feel a little crazy? What if

these words of endearment are spoken in the morning, then your partner brings a friend home for the evening without advance consultation, and you have neither the energy nor the inclination to be enter-
taining.

The scenarios are infinite. Who "I" am keeps shifting and who
"he" or "she" is does as well. Which is the real "you"? Which are the
true feelings? Is it safer to avoid the verbal commitment and not later
have to meet ambivalence head on?

If the words are spoken too often, do they lose their meaning? Or
do they serve as an important reminder, especially in the bad times?
Does saying those words come more easily to people of some ethnic
heritages than others? Do the French and the Italians speak more
freely of their love, and if so, does that mean they are indeed more
sincerely loving, or less?

A world of questions. I can only conclude that for some the words
bring discomfort, and for others great pleasure and reassurance. And
for many, they may have lost all special meaning and become as pro
forma as simply saying *good-bye*.

I rarely speak those words, though sometimes I write them, and
then I mean them most sincerely. I, after all, was married to a man
named Larsen, whose ancestors came from a northern land of short
days and long winter nights. I fondly recall the day he turned to me
with a wry smile and asked if I'd heard the one about the Norwegian
farmer who loved his wife so much, he almost told her.

Word Power

U.S. Supreme Court Justice Hugo Black, staunch defender of the First Amendment, never wrote a free speech decision I didn't like.

From my perspective, even symbolic speech---armbands worn by protesting high school students, flag burning---should be protected. We should willingly expose all that is spoken or written or symbolized to the light of day and encourage conversation in the "free market place of ideas." I reject not only government censorship but most institutional voluntary censorship as well. Of course, I make exceptions for speech or symbols that create a clear and present danger (i.e. shouting "fire" in a crowded theater), and for protection of youngsters from material deemed too frightening or perverse, but little else.

So that's my public stance. But there's another aspect to my story.

Recently two of my colleagues were chatting in my office about a judicial ruling, and one said, "He didn't have the balls to . . ." For two seconds I stopped breathing. I turned to the non-speaker and asked, "Are you surprised she used those words?"

"Of course not," he replied jovially. "I use language like that and far worse, although never in front of you."

By now we were all consumed with laughter, but mine was a bit uneasy.

Yes, I know all the words, and I suffer through their endless use in modern film, literature and overheard cell phone conversations. But they have never been part of my vocabulary, and without my asking them, perceptive friends and family protect my ears.

My public position on free speech and my private reaction do not match. It's a good illustration of cognitive dissonance, a disconnect: My emotional response belies my intellectual outlook. Will I be perceived as protesting too much by insisting that I am not a prude? I am not. So, why this inconsistency?

Swear words that don't reference an almighty being typically allude to sexual or bodily functions. For generations younger than mine, repeated usage of these words has robbed them of all shock value and probably of any real meaning. They're just a way to let off steam.

Formerly the province of boys and men, girls and women are entering the fray using them too. Are they letting the world know they are "one of the boys"?

"Forbidden" words are more than expletives. When someone speaks them in my presence, they cross my privacy boundary, evoking unwanted, uninvited crude images. In some instances they make the beautiful ugly. Is this why for me, but not for most others, they carry the negative impact they do? Perhaps.

Will my new insight bring about a shift, a relaxation? Actually over time, I have loosened up a bit. But will those words ever fall easily from my lips?

Not likely.

At a Loss for Words

My friend was in a quandary, and when he told me what had happened, I joined him in his loss for words. For both of us, our livelihood calls upon our facility with language, but we were at sea.

Here's the story: A few weeks ago he went to lunch with a colleague---we'll call him Stan---who had just come from a business meeting where an important matter was being negotiated. The only woman at the table raised serious questions about a position taken by Stan, and his anger, though controlled, had flared.

Afterward, he met my friend for lunch, and as they slid into the restaurant booth, Stan remarked, "These lesbians can be relentless," with a jocular, *if you know what I mean* grin. My friend was silent.

They ordered lunch and the discussion shifted. The derisive comment was allowed to simply evaporate without rejoinder.

But my friend's discomfort did not evaporate, for weeks later, he and I sat talking and wondering how he might have (and should have) countered that remark. We both have friends, colleagues and family members who are gay or lesbian, and were offended and angered revisiting that scene. Yet, we were at a loss for the words that he might have spoken in response. Oh, we had no trouble designing cutting insults that would have embarrassed Stan, or labeling him a bigot. But Stan was someone with whom my friend would continue to work. And even if he were not, an aggressive remark that would have added to the discomfort of the moment was not in my friend's repertoire. Yet by remaining silent, he felt he had lacked courage and been defeated.

If the goal is to raise consciousness, then simply confronting or demeaning might just harden beliefs and enhance a defensive posture. Another approach is needed.

I've taken a survey of sorts, asked many friends how they would respond to an ugly remark, a pejorative identity statement. None could offer a rejoinder that worked, at least from my perspective. Most had experienced similar conversations and also remained silent, at best making their point by walking away, if the setting allowed.

After much thought and some reading (including the fine book *Taking the War Out of Our Words* by Sharon Strand Ellison), I've come up with a sound approach. A bigoted remark can be addressed with a non-defensive question, one that simply seeks further exploration of the person's meaning. The question must express genuine curiosity and be non-accusatory. And it must be asked in an open, non-critical tone, an inflection that sincerely invites a thoughtful response, like *Stan, tell me why you think that's so.*

If he responds in the same disparaging vein, at least a conversation has begun, and the way is open to a sharing of experience and knowledge. Expressing genuine curiosity would appear to be the key.

On the other hand, Stan might simply answer, *I guess that was a pretty crude remark on my part.* Then, a simple yes in response would suffice, with perhaps a smile as well.

Don't Assume, Ask

Too often I've assumed others shared my point of view, only to later learn how wrong I was. Why does it matter?

Communication is the heart of a good relationship. But if our perception about how another is thinking or feeling is off, and we don't know it (or choose to avoid knowing it), we're starting the slide into misunderstanding and away from intimacy.

An almost comical (if not so poignant) example often comes to mind. In 2000, my husband and I sold the home in which we'd lived for more than forty years and raised our family. Len had been diagnosed with Parkinson's three years earlier, and although his symptoms were still mild, he was finding climbing stairs ever more arduous. So we decided to move.

To our great good fortune, we found a sunny apartment rental with a river view, a parking garage, and no stairs. Our house sold quickly, and we simplified life by downsizing our possessions. Both of us felt lighthearted to be leaving so much responsibility behind.

For me, raised in and around New York City, the return to apartment life was like putting on a pair of comfortable old shoes. Len had grown up roaming the open prairies of Illinois, but for five years soon after we married, we had lived in one flat or another when he attended Columbia University, and he'd relished city life.

So, we happily settled into our new seventh-floor home, with only ourselves to please, unencumbered but for our cat, Eleanor. Hers, it seemed, was the major adjustment, for she went from a life of wandering and hunting outdoors, to a life completely circumscribed by the apartment walls and a small balcony.

When our first visitors inquired about how we enjoyed our new living quarters, I readily answered for both of us that it was all quite wonderful. Len just smiled.

Then Eleanor padded into the room, and they asked how she was adjusting to being an indoor cat.

"She loves it," I said.

"She hates it," Len offered on the heels of my comment. "She feels trapped and confined."

I was shocked. We were both projecting our feelings onto our inscrutable cat. Quite unconsciously, I'd attributed to my own emotional state an objective reality Len did not share. While I was comforted and delighted with our new surroundings, he felt an unspoken despair as his world continued to narrow and his physical limitations advanced.

I should have asked him instead of assuming he shared my positive response to our move.

Ironically, openly assigning our feelings to our furry pet launched important conversations. I needed to face what he, until that moment, had hidden, and what I'd preferred not to know.

Intimacy was renewed.

Schmooze or Lose

I usually avoid large social gatherings (defined as more than five people) and even family get-togethers where small talk is likely to be the order of the day. My firmly held belief has long been that unless conversation is sincerely self-disclosing or purposeful, it is a waste of time. I applied this standard both to social events and to professional meetings. But that was then, and this is now. I have since become a believer in the power of schmooze.

If you have not yet read *Beyond Reason* by Roger Fisher (of *Getting to Yes* fame) and his co-author, psychologist David Shapiro, put it on your list. It gave me a valuable new perspective on the importance of making a personal connection (affiliation) with others to establish a positive emotional climate for a negotiation. The sub-title of this book is *Using Emotion as You Negotiate*. Written in the style of *Getting to Yes*, it is a quick and worthy read, replete with the authors' own experiences, both professional and personal.

Whether it is with a legal adversary, a partner, a spouse, or even a teenager, are we not all in negotiation mode at some time of almost every day?

The authors identify five universal core concerns that, if attended to, will foster a positive emotional response and, if ignored, will likely thwart a good outcome. The first is "build affiliation." When we meet with someone we will be working with, the authors advise us to find some common ground or experience: the school your children attend, your approaching retirements, a movie you both happened to see, the neighborhood in which you live, or if all else fails (and only if all else fails), sports or the weather. Sharing common experiences creates a sense of connection, something we all yearn for (even if we do not acknowledge it) and sets a positive emotional climate for the work that will follow.

The authors address four more equally important universal core concerns, but I will not discuss them here, so read the book---you will not regret it. Still, if you have any doubts about the value of schmoozing because you too are an introvert and are small-talk avoidant, read on.

Janice Nadler of the law school faculty at Northwestern University, and her co-authors, conducted an experiment with graduate management students. Each Northwestern student was paired with a student at a distant school to take part in a negotiation simulation by e-mail. All the participants were given their partner's name and contact information, as well as a set of facts presenting a complex problem that they were to negotiate together over a three-day period. On the day that the negotiation was to begin, half of the pairs were told to conduct a brief (no more than five minute) preliminary phone conversation. They were not to refer to the facts of the problem in any way, but were simply to engage in small talk, get minimally acquainted, perhaps chat about their respective schools, cities, family, even the weather if they chose, but nothing particularly purposeful. Then for three days they negotiated the given problem. Those who had had the insignificant friendly exchange the day before went on to achieve agreement four times as often as those who had not.

Those preliminary calls of little substantive import, Fisher and Shapiro would no doubt agree, had built affiliation by forming a personal connection and had the effect of reducing personal distance between the negotiating partners. The brief casual exchanges seemed to allow the students to achieve far greater success.

I have to shift gears, stop complaining, and improve my schmoozing skills. But in a strictly social setting, keeping the time spent on small talk under five minutes still seems like a fine idea.

Just Don't Ask

There are times when personal experience informs professional practice. This is the story of one of those times.

My husband was of Norwegian descent. He wrote with eloquence, but except when teaching or working with his students, he was a man of few words who could comfortably go for long periods without speaking at all. In the early years of our marriage, I was often unsure whether his silence conveyed unhappiness. So I would probe, ask a question, and then another, but at these times his sparse responses served to close, not open, the door to understanding.

When I talked of this with a psychologist friend, she said, "You need to learn some new dance steps. Stop asking questions. Just tell him something about yourself, only a few sentences, and make no accusations. See what happens."

It worked. A brief back-and-forth began, and he shared a few important words. The next day I repeated my new steps, and a bit more disclosure followed, and we both were more at ease.

Recently, the occasion arose for me to offer this wisdom to another.

A newly separated husband and wife, parents to a seven-year-old daughter, were seated on my office couch. At the start of his assigned weekends with the child, the father would pick her up at school. Despite his efforts to engage her in conversation, she was unwilling to talk with him in any meaningful way. He accused his wife of turning their daughter against him, believing that it was all her doing.

First I asked him to recount a typical attempt at conversation.

He: "Hi sweetie, how was your day? "

She: "Fine."

He: "Learn anything new?"

She: "Not much."

He: "Any good friends in your class?"

She: "Maybe."

He: "So, play with them today?"

She: "Yes."

He: "What sort of games?"

She: "Oh, just stuff."

Frustrated, he would shut down, angry and hurt, and they would ride along in silence until they reached his home, where his daughter would shower affection on the dog, turn on the TV, and cuddle with her pet. He felt like an outsider. This conversation dance would repeat many times during the visit.

It's hard to know what this youngster's feelings were when she left school with her father instead of returning to the parent with whom she was perhaps more comfortable. What subliminal message from her mother did she carry? Did his being the one who left their home feel to her like abandonment? Did she wonder if she was at fault for her parents' separation? There's no easy way for a seven-year-old to address these issues even to herself. Was closing the door on his questions a perfect defense against revealing a confusion of emotions?

Bringing to mind my past experience with a sometimes-silent partner, I suggested, "Try this: Stop asking questions. Just talk about yourself, nothing too profound and not accusing or in any way critical. Maybe talk about what happened to you earlier in the day. But no questions."

When he arrived for the next visit to my office, he was smiling. "Amazing!" he reported. "I picked her up at school. No questions. Told her about the pizza I had for lunch, made with anchovies, which I hate, and what a time I had dislodging them from the layers of cheese. She told me about the yucky salmon patties served in the school cafeteria and how one of the boys started tossing them around and got into trouble. She said she knew his older sister, who was stuck up. So I told her about a woman in my office who was stuck up, and she asked why I thought people got that way. We had a great talk."

No monumental disclosures were made, but tensions eased, and the possibility of real talk was there again.

So refraining from asking questions of those who are withdrawn, young and old alike, and telling your own story, may be the best step to take.

CHAPTER TWO

EXPECTATIONS

Fairness: An Unrealistic Expectation

It is wonderful to engage with someone who has worked their way out of despair and become optimistic about the future.

The enthusiastic woman I met with was participating in divorce mediation and preparing a counter-proposal for her husband. After completing several months of obviously useful therapy, she had given up lamenting the past and was facing the end of her marriage with newfound courage, determined to convince her soon-to-be former spouse to amend his most recent proposal for support.

The background story: this wife had earned a library science degree a decade ago, but now that her status as the stay-at-home parent would soon be over, she had a new career goal that required a return to school. For her to implement this plan, her husband would need to contribute to her support for a longer period than he had offered.

Her plea to him some months ago was, "Before the kids were even born, we agreed that I would leave work and stay home full time to give them a good start. Now it's only fair for you to pay for my return to school."

His response was, "True, that was the agreement we made, but it was never contemplated that you would switch careers. The fair thing is for you to help bring in income now."

When fairness is the goal and each party asks the other "to be fair", what they really are saying is: *If you saw the world as I do, then you would agree with me. Since you don't, you're unfair.*

Pleas for fairness, a subjective concept, typically fall on deaf ears. Bargaining for fairness simply pushes people further apart, making them less likely to reach agreement. The conversation ends. So, when you know where you want to go but keep tripping up along the way, it's time to take a different tack, to be strategic.

This newly empowered woman was no longer stuck in the fairness trap. Still legitimately negotiating to meet her self-interest, she now said to her husband, "With additional training, I could achieve a far better salary and feel a sense of real satisfaction in my work. If you help me accomplish this, I'd commit to paying a portion of the kid's future college tuition, as you've been asking. Would you be willing to consider this?"

Maybe when life is turned upside down, we all regress to some extent, and as a child might whine with the stamp of a foot, insist, "It's just not fair."

But once it is clear what it is you want and why, the strategic approach is to state what you are willing to offer in return---for example to say: If I offered you ABC, would you be willing to consider giving me XYZ? This approach has the added benefit of suggesting an interest in consulting on the solution, which acknowledges that the other person has a position worthy of respect. A genuine show of respect always keeps the conversation moving forward.

A reciprocal offer trumps a plea for fairness every time.

When the Unknown Matters

It was clear to her the marriage should end. He disagreed, but reluctantly he acquiesced, and they entered mediation.

Oddly, when describing the nature of their day-to-day lives, he and she did not differ. I puzzled over how they could portray even the details of their circumstances in the very same way yet reach such different conclusions.

They had two youngsters. That was reason enough for me to probe, to question whether they might still take another direction. Perhaps they'd be open to working with a counselor.

When I met alone with the husband, he acknowledged there had been some rough times and told me, without any obvious emotion, that there had been no physical intimacy for well over a year. They talked little, he said, but they seldom fought and rarely were at odds about the children. Somberly, he said, "So, it isn't all that bad."

When I met alone with his wife, I shared with her what he had said. Her response was immediate and animated. She told me that his parents remained married, although they were miserable with each other and had been for years. They slept in separate bedrooms, and hardly spoke. "That's their life," she said, "but not the life I intend to live."

I asked about her own parents' marriage. She smiled and sat back, her taut body relaxing. She described it as comfortable and loving, telling of tender moments between them that she often witnessed as a child.

Now I understood why these partners had reached such opposite conclusions about the viability of their marriage.

Marriages fail for varied and complex reasons. In this one, neither partner was willing or able to appreciate the other's view of what a marriage should be. We see the world through our own lens, and only with deliberate effort do we look through the lens of another. Would

things have been otherwise for this couple if they had sought help early on and come to recognize the importance of their unique family
histories? With that understanding, might they have tried to recapture
and build upon what had initially drawn them together? But it's impossible to know. Perhaps they are an extreme example of what everyone making a commitment faces, whether aware of it or not: the
model of marriage that seeped into their partner's consciousness when
young.

When a loved one communicates disapproval or unhappiness to
you, consider this: Before disappointment ripens into disdain, ask,
with genuine interest (free of sarcasm), "Tell me what you expected."
And then really listen to the answer. Let it be the basis for self-
disclosing conversations. Talk about what you both hoped for and
what accommodations you both might make once you understand
each other's outlook. Or perhaps make a well-considered decision not
to accommodate, but make the effort to learn how best to live with
your differences.

It is said the road to hell is paved with good intentions. More likely
it is paved with unrealistic expectations, never explored until it is too
late.

The Talking Cure, Unfinished

It was some time ago that Evelyn phoned. Unhappy for several years, she told me she was contemplating divorce, but remained unsure. Her speech was halting and her tone subdued. The children were grown and on their own, and she spoke of being seized with anxiety imagining a future alone

She described her husband, Hank, sympathetically, as a good man who was downhearted as well but unwilling to consider marriage counseling. I encouraged her not to leave the counseling decision to him alone and to consider working with a therapist on her own.

Months later Hank called to schedule mediation, reminding me of the earlier call from Evelyn. He said he was actually the one who had finally made the decision to end the marriage.

A week later when they entered my office, Evelyn's bright smile projected surprising self-assurance. Proudly she announced that she had completed therapy, and her self-respect had been restored. It seemed an apparent success story, but it was not. Evelyn's posture, and the words she now chose, reflected a determination to be assertive on her own behalf. She hardly seemed the same woman I'd talked with before. But my smile, although congratulatory, was not quite wholehearted. Something was off.

As we explored the data they had gathered and identified the issues to be resolved, Evelyn laced her comments with sarcasm, directing a few sharp personal insults at her husband. Hank's jaw tightened, his face grim. Therapy, and perhaps other events of which I had no knowledge, had certainly fostered change, but was it for the better?

I often met with divorcing parties who, like Evelyn, have worked with a counselor, gained confidence, and come to honor their new sense of self by speaking in a new way. Sometimes their statements are tinged with anger long repressed. Their determination to no longer endure unhappy circumstances suggests they underwent a significant catharsis. Many are then better able to serve their own interests. But for some, their newfound assurance edges into belligerence, and their effort to negotiate a good outcome fails.

I'm tempted to offer Evelyn unsolicited advice, but I know it would neither be welcome nor wise. We all see the world through the lens of past experience, that which is known to us, and that which is hidden from view but influential nonetheless. It would be presumptuous of me, looking through my lens, to advise. But next time we meet, I will pose some questions for Evelyn and in private share my experience. As she embraces her new-found strength, I ask myself, must Hank be diminished, denigrated?

Therapy often helps us to recognize and dissect actions of our parents that we may have translated into grievances. With maturity we come to accept, even forgive, their human frailties along with our own. But with an intimate partner, being able to forgive the failure of love is more of a challenge, especially if one feels rejected and the wounds are so exposed in the here and now

A partner's most valuable resource for achieving a positive negotiated outcome, one that costs nothing in a monetary sense, is genuine respect for the other. Yet, so often it is the most difficult thing to offer when a marriage is ending.

I will ask Evelyn: "Would you be willing to return to counseling to seek an understanding of the roots of your anger, to go beyond your personal validation?"

Respect is the key, but not self-respect alone.

The Risks of Optimism

I am an optimist, most of the time. But recent research suggests that optimists don't predict future outcomes as well as their depressed brothers and sisters. So what meaning does this have for me and my fellow enthusiasts? Daniel Kahneman, an economics professor at Princeton and Nobel laureate, has said, of mistakes made by overly optimistic executives: "People assign much higher probability to the truth of their opinions than is warranted...a natural inclination to exaggerate our talents is amplified by a tendency to misperceive the causes of events. The typical pattern is for people to take credit for positive outcomes and to attribute negative outcomes to external factors, no matter what their true cause." I thought this a valuable insight, clipped the article, and put it aside.

Later, when a mediation I was conducting failed, it came back to mind. The husband was a successful business executive, whose wife saw his actions and heard his statements as blaming and threatening. A musician, she perceived herself as the victim of his intimidating ways, and in our sessions emotionally withdrew, unable or unwilling to assert her own interests.It became clear that the husband's bullying ways, and the wife's retreat to tears and silence, made their negotiation problematic, so I terminated the sessions.

Now, remembering Kahneman's insight, I was asking myself whether my decision was wise. He suggests that one way to improve on decision-making is to systematically analyze our mistakes. But he thinks business managers are likely to resist adopting procedures that would be threatening to them.

My colleagues and I love to talk about our successful outcomes, especially in cases that presented unusual challenges. And we frequently consult with one another when faced with a difficult case and suggest alternative strategies. But seldom do we devote much time to systematically analyzing our failures, except to note the external causes. I can often identify my mistakes, and I am comfortable apologizing for them. But I spend little time seriously considering how I might have handled a situation differently. Is there too much discomfort in that?

Perhaps CEOs with an eye on the Dow Jones believe they must avoid disclosing mistakes lest the value of their stock decline. But my asking what did I do wrong and how might I have done this differently, is an analysis my colleagues and I can keep quite private.

So, I've even decided to step across the boundary from my professional to my personal life and pose the same questions when my optimistic plans go awry.

Will the Prince Be Charming?

They were young but had finished high school before they married. That's the good news. The bad news is that after seventeen years, the marriage is over.

But there is much more good news. They have two teenage daughters who are gracefully weathering adolescence, saddened by the family turmoil but still high achieving and with a loving connection to both parents. The parents, for their part, take great pride in them. The husband lauds his wife as a wonderful mother and credits her with their children's success.

After working only at home for fifteen years, she recently found part-time employment. They are in complete agreement that the girls should continue to have parental attention, even now. Especially now. So she will keep her new job and remain available to manage and monitor the girls' busy after-school hours.

He owns a few shares of a small but profitable family business where he works, and he is destined to take over when his father retires and gradually gifts him the remaining stock. His hard work has yielded income seven times his wife's modest salary, and they are financially solvent.

And still more good news. Although he is the one who has chosen to leave, he speaks of his determination to remain on friendly terms with his soon-to-be former wife and, no matter what it takes, to be fair. Prince Charming is resolute and insists he will not disappoint.

So, although she is a bit tearful---sad and frightened about a future alone---she is repeatedly promised, "All will be well."

But now, for the worst news: The meaning of "all will be well".
He assures her that her current standard of living will be maintained as long as there is a child living at home, and perhaps for a couple of years beyond that, six years in all. Her lawyer says this term of years is generous. And during this time, her husband will provide more sup-

port than the court would order. All of their property will be equally divided, a bit of equity in their home and his modest 401(k). So, why is this bad news? Calmed and breathing more easily, she asks, "What about the business?"

"Well, you know," he says, "my grandfather started it and passed it down to my father, so one day it will be mine."

"But for seventeen years I took care of everything so you could devote yourself to building the business. We should own that together, right?"

Wrong.

They both seek advice from their lawyers and learn that the small stock ownership interest already gifted to him may have some marital value to share, but not much. It would be minimal compared to the value of the business asset he will one day own.

Realization dawns on her. Angry now and in tears, she says, "When you were working fourteen-hour days, I didn't complain because it was for all of us. Now you will always be secure, probably even rich! After six years I'll barely be able to survive!"

This is where the story ends, for now. To be continued, as there are more conversations to be had and decisions to be made.

If I could write the script, this wife, while still being supported will spend the next six years in school, and regain the power she gave away when she auditioned for and landed the role of Cinderella. Her prince is charming, will continue to work hard, and likely pay their daughters' college expenses.

But now it is up to her to design the rest of her life, so as never to be so wholly dependent again.

Daughters everywhere: Are you getting the message?

Jill Ker Conway

By chance, I happened upon a CNN panel discussion and heard the words of an old friend I've never met. That's not an impossibility, if we've experienced the world of that person through their own telling, in print.

Jill Ker Conway became well known to me over fifteen years ago when I read the story of her early life. She is now a woman in her eighties, retired as President of Smith College and a visiting scholar at M.I.T.

In *The Road From Coorain* Conway tells of her youth growing up in Australia. After World War II, her father homesteaded vast acreage in the Outback, where the entire family took part in raising sheep for wool. Unlike her two older brothers, who had been sent off to boarding schools, she grew to age eleven without ever attending a formal school, although, interestingly, she was raised with the expectation that she would become equally as competent (a message I too received from both parents).

Even as sand storms howled around their ranch home, miles from the nearest neighbor, her mother laid her evening table with linen, silver and crystal, as caught up as most Australians of her generation in allegiance to the standards of the British upper class. Valiant in her support of her husband and young family as they dealt with the adversity of a prolonged devastating drought and extreme heat, she delivered mixed messages to Jill about what it meant to be a woman. Modeling great strength and expecting high academic achievement, she also offered her daughter not-so-subtle advice to hide her intelligence in order to be popular with young men (messages I too received).

Following the premature death of her father, the Ker family moved to Sidney, and in 1958 Jill graduated from the university with highest honors. But she was denied the employment opportunities offered to her male colleagues and fully wakened to the dichotomy of the treatment of men and women. (In 1969, the year of my graduation, law firms in the U.S. hired no women attorneys.)

Eventually Conway immigrated to the United States as a history scholar and continued her graduate education, becoming a renowned educator and author of many acclaimed books.

Conway and I also share a historical context. When I read her next volume of autobiography, *True North*, I was able to compare how we experienced the radicalization of many women in the 1960s and 1970s and the changes since that time. The ardent demands of those years are now commonplace expectations. Young girls today are born to these expectations and have no need to be covert in their behaviors.

Reading about the real life of another, hearing her voice, illuminates our own life. I will likely never meet Jill Ker Conway, but I know her well, and she has helped to give my world definition.

Standing Alone

My brother, a college professor, told me about his graduate students who were struggling to make important decisions about their futures. The stress of indecision was taking its toll on them. The conundrum: Should they take the not-quite-right job, or continue with their education and incur more debt? They feared making a choice they might later regret. Still in their twenties, most of them stood alone in the face of uncertainty.

So different from my experience, back in the 1940s. I can think of only two significant choices I made on my own, outside the orbit of parental influence: at seventeen, where to go to college, then at twenty, whether to marry.

Once I was married, for the next fifty-three years, I made virtually every major choice in concert with someone who was equally invested in my future. Not that the issues Len and I faced were simple, but we would share the impact of each decision, and we knew we could fall back into each other's comforting ways if things went awry. And that made a difference.

Now I'm once again making decisions on my own, but I'm comfortable doing so, drawing upon a lifetime of experience. But most young people today, who postpone serious personal commitments and remain independent far into their twenties or even thirties, are called upon to make important choices without much decision-making experience.

My brother wanted to show his students that rarely is there only one right answer, and that even if we make a wrong decision, we can deal with it and make corrections. So he told them two simple stories from his past.

Back in the 1940s, when he was only fourteen, his first paying job was sorting potato chips. It's hard to imagine in this automated age. He was told to grade each chip as to quality and size, then push it into one of four separate bins. During his early days on the job, he repeat-edly was unable to decide on the proper category for a particular chip, so he asked his boss, who told him, "Bruce, you are simply going to have to make these decisions." So he did, without any negative rami-fications.

Many years later, with a recent PhD in hand, he worked in a phys-ics laboratory in Princeton, New Jersey. His research team was look-ing for a new hire, and he took part in the interviewing process. He favored one particular candidate and approached his superior, urging him to select this one, only to have his choice rejected. He persisted, arguing the merits of his favorite applicant, and finally wore his boss down. "Okay, Bruce," his boss told him, "but I'm telling you here and now, you'll have to take full responsibility for this decision."

My brother agreed, reasoning that if his pick worked out well, he would get all the credit. If he didn't work out, what was his boss going to do, go to his superiors and tell them he'd turned the hiring decision over to someone else? Not likely. At worst the boss would tell him he'd made a bad call. That was a risk he was willing to take.

These stories, and the conversations they generated with his stu-dents, were his way of encouraging them to get their feet wet in the responsibility waters, wanting to assure them that that's not nearly as frightening as it seems from dry land.

Since my brother's early decision-making days, and my own, risk analysis has been elevated to a science of sorts. Will it help these young folks who stand alone to jump from the edge of the future abyss into their next steps? Perhaps, but how nice it would be if there were loving arms to break their fall.

Fairy Tales

I met my new mediation clients as they stepped off the elevator and guided them to my office door. Their smiles were broad. Usually I see signs of apprehension on the faces of those who arrive to unravel the fabric of their marriage, but not in this case.

As they became comfortable seated on opposite ends of my couch, she said, "It's hard to believe we're here. It was supposed to be happily ever after."

I smiled, for I too grew up loving fairy tales.

"We just want to be fair to each other," he said. "I want her to be financially secure and she wants me to be able to start a new career."

They glanced at each other with approval, conveying gratitude for their mutual understanding. Then they sat forward, eager to begin.

"What does financial security mean for you?" I asked her.

"Well, staying in the house with the kids. We both want that."

He nodded, and I asked him, "Will that be possible if you leave your job?"

"Sure," he said. "When she cashes in her share of my retirement account and adds to that what she can earn, they'll be able to stay put for a least a year."

She appeared confused. "Wait---that's not my plan. That's not fair."

"Why not?" he said. "What about being fair to me?"

I'd not yet heard their full story, but I saw that another myth would soon be proved false, that they would agree on what was fair. It was already clear that what one thought would be a fair outcome was not close to being fair from the perspective of the other. Their plans no longer meshed. Although they shared many values, they inevitably did not share all of them.

I offered my view that when a marriage is ending, seeking a mutual sense of fairness is an ever-elusive goal, one best abandoned. Puzzled, and disheartened, they sat back.

I wanted to reassure them but not create false expectations, so told them that I urge mediation clients to adopt a flea market mentality. Finding an item you wish to purchase, you ask the dealer, "How much?"

And if the dealer says the price is twenty dollars, you don't say, "But that's not fair."

You might offer to pay ten dollars and then settle for fifteen. The deal is not struck by arguing the fairness of the price but by reaching an acceptable one.

It is futile to try to convince someone to agree with your sense of fairness when their values (or perceptions) differ from your own. The key to success is for the negotiating partners to probe each other's underlying interests in achieving their stated goals. Why is it important to her to remain in a home now too large and expensive? Why is it important to him to immediately leave his present job? That conversation would surely unlock their imagination.

Eventually they developed many options to consider. She will seek to provide some additional income. He will postpone leaving his job while looking for another. They will likely decide to sell the house after all.

When I tell this story to a friend, she chides me for being cynical.

"Not cynical," I said, "but pragmatic."

She persists: "Fairness is when you'd call it fair if you were in the other person's shoes. That's achievable and worth striving for."

I'm unconvinced.

To yearn for fairness may be a good thing if it promotes compromise. But to expect agreement on what a fair outcome would be is folly. Realistically, there is no such thing as objective fairness except perhaps in tales from the Brothers Grimm.

A Perfectly Good Frog

A woman in her mid-fifties tells me a familiar story. After much thought, she has decided to end her 30-year marriage. Disappointed, she yearned for a truly intimate relationship, one that offers greater sharing of feelings and experiences. The husband she describes was someone she still respects and cares about, and there had been neither infidelity nor a clash of values. But she is terribly lonely within what outsiders see as a happy marriage.

As I listen, I wonder about the expectations with which she grew up.

Do young people today believe that the person they choose as a lifetime partner will forever meet all of their needs? That was the myth of my youth, literally a fairytale that I first heard from the Brothers Grimm. It was perpetuated by romantic films and certainly by parents, who feared (before the pill) that their daughters might not wait for Prince Charming. Now that most marriages are postponed a few years and partners are more mature and relationship savvy, has that myth changed? Not from my vantage point.

Len and I never stopped seeking the comfort and pleasure of physical closeness, but over time, though not without significant angst (and an occasional resort to the talking cure), we learned to appreciate our differences, and to actually foster each other's independence. Although we had a rich life together, we also enjoyed many friends and experiences we did not share. My earlier assumption that in marriage we would achieve perfect togetherness faded. And a good thing too.

When a friend or client tells me they are thinking about ending an otherwise good relationship because the desired level of emotional intimacy is lacking, they seem to hope, even to anticipate, that they will be able to find the complete closeness they are yearning for with a new partner.

Hearing this, I harbor a concern that their search for this idealized love will fail.

We put a great burden on our mate, to be all things to us, to fill each and every need. But we might be better served by calling upon others when lonely times arise. The road to hell is paved with unrealistic expectations.

On my desk I have a cartoon in which Madame Gilda, the fortune teller, is being asked by the seeker of her supernatural powers: "How can I save my marriage?"

Madame Gilda answers, as she consults her crystal ball: "Stop trying to turn a perfectly good frog into a prince!"

CHAPTER THREE

FAMILY

About Fathers

Time was, not all that long ago, when Father brought home the bacon, and Mother (while rocking the cradle) cooked it in the pan. But today, neither fathers nor mothers are who they once were. As new doors opened for women, men's lives have changed as well.

Some of my close friends are coming for brunch on Father's Day to talk about our fathers, the part they played in who we became, and how they influenced our relationships with our partners, our children, and authority figures. Did we strive to perpetuate what we thought positive and mindfully try to avoid repeating the negative? Were we successful?

The three fathers in my life were Len's, mine, and of course, Len as a father.

Len faced adversity many times, but I witnessed his unrestrained tears only at the funeral of his father, a man of Norwegian heritage, usually stern of face. His father had grown up poor with a commanding work ethic, an intellectual with only an eighth-grade education. In the years I knew him, he was an electrician for the railroad and even in his sixties labored outside in Chicago's cruel winter temperatures. Devoted and loyal to his wife and family, but undemonstrative, he was a man of few words and those were often critical. A self-taught pianist, photographer and grower of exquisite flowers, he expressed pleasure in these endeavors and a sensuality that otherwise, even with close family members, seemed absent.

I always thought of him as trapped inside himself.

His son's tearful regret was never having told his father he loved him.

When his own children were young, Len was a tender and affectionate father. He fed and bathed them and got them to bed three nights a week for four years, while I attended evening law school. Later, as the 1970s approached, he struggled to adjust to the social turmoil: his sons' hair length, raucous protests of the Vietnam War on the university campus and sexual mores turned upside down. Tensions rose in our family, especially with our adolescent sons. Len's anger was visible but repressed. He was, in a sense, at war with himself, believing in two opposite truths, the standards with which he had been raised but also in the new freedoms unfolding.

Years later, in our children's early adulthood, Len purposely sought to reestablish closeness with his sons. He took each of them alone on canoeing treks into the wilderness, or on cross-country flights in his small plane, resolved to speak of and assure the parental love and approval he had so longed for, and wanting to be known for who he was in the present.

As to my own father, I regret not having come to know him better. I asked too few questions. Self-absorbed as an adolescent and then preoccupied with my own growing family and developing career, we seldom had private moments for intimate conversations when we visited. My mother was ever present, her persona more vivid. As a young teenager, my father traveled to America on his own to join other family members escaping the pogroms in tsarist Russia. He arrived speaking no English, but ten years later earned a law degree at New York University. He was off to work early and returned home late during the Depression years, and even thereafter, so most of my childhood memories of him are indistinct, as a kind and quiet presence, often humming some unrecognizable tune.

When at home, I remember him reading, away from the center of activity. My parents' love for each other seemed ever present, expressed in the way they spoke and often touched. Troubling words either went unsaid or more likely were voiced behind closed doors.

I never told my father I loved him, but for that I have no regret, only gratitude for our having been so secure in our love for each other. His approval of me, even if unspoken, was evident in the warmth of his smile each time we met.

Some of my friends tell of fathers who were autocratic, disapproving, and even cruel. Today I watch them with their loved ones and witness tenderness, devotion, and respect. I marvel at how they have reversed the tide and wonder if their fathers too were trapped inside themselves.

The greatest gift the women's movement gave to men was to move over and make room for them in the lives of their children, to nurture and know them and be known by them.

But how many of us think we know our fathers as well as we know our mothers?

Mother Always Loved You Best

The woman's name announced over my office intercom was vaguely familiar. As I lifted the phone, she said, "You may not remember me. It's been seven years since I, my mother, and my sister worked with you. Now my sister is dying and refuses to see me. Can you help?"

I remember my failed mediations more vividly than my successes, so as soon as she offered this bit of background, I remembered her well.

Some years ago a friend of a friend had called me to ask if I could mediate a problem that was tearing her family apart. Months earlier, having reached the age of eighty-five, she had disclosed to her daughters that she planned to leave her sizable estate to them in equal shares.

The older daughter lived on the West Coast, divorced and without children; she had achieved considerable success in the film industry and was financially secure. Although fully engaged in a demanding career, she had maintained close contact with her mother.

Her sister, a gifted student in high school and college, had married young. She and her professionally trained husband raised five children on a small subsistence farm, home schooling their youngsters. Neither had pursued paid employment. The mother lived nearby so witnessed the unmet needs of her younger daughter's family and regularly helped out financially, eventually even paying the college expenses of her grandchildren. Over many years she had contributed a substantial sum, never tallied.

The older sister had always accepted her sibling's life choices without rancor, but believed, from comments her mother had made in the past, that in the end a balance would be struck. She expected to receive a larger share of the estate. Now she was incensed. Her memory of that understanding was questioned.

Family discussions became frequent and bitter. The mother wavered. Her every effort to soothe anger or develop a compromise solution only evoked more anger from one daughter or the other. She was distraught. I agreed to try to help, and the three women came to my office. The chill between the sisters, both in their early sixties, was starkly evident. Grim-faced, they avoided eye contact and looked past each other even when in the same room.

I conducted two lengthy mediation sessions, to no avail. Despite developing a number of options that could to some extent address the unequal gifting, the sisters remained positional, both insisting they were standing on principle. The older demanded a year-to-year accounting of the contributions their mother had made to the younger and her family. The younger flatly refused to develop such a record and was adamant there be no change from the plan for equal shares. Both addressed their mother's anxiety and sadness with loving gestures but no deference. They spurned my suggestion that they meet with a family therapist. Whenever someone says, "It's not about the money, just the principle involved," I raise a cynical eyebrow.

In this situation, however, it really didn't seem to be about the money. It seemed to be about preferential love. The sisters seemed to me to be allowing old childhood jealousies and rivalries for affection and approval to sweep in and supplant mature behavior, even at the expense of the physical and emotional well-being of their beloved elderly parent. Barring mental incompetence or significant evidence of undue influence, neither of which was suggested here, parents are entitled to autonomy and respect for whatever decisions they make about how they use their assets during their lifetime and the disposition of their estate, are they not?

This story does not have a happy ending. I later learned that the mother died without changing her plan to leave her estate in equal shares. Since then neither daughter had spoken to the other. Then the younger sister developed a terminal illness, and the older sister wished to visit and make amends.

That was when the older sister called me. At her request, I made an offer of intervention, but the younger sister did not accept it.

I tried to stand in the shoes of each daughter and wonder why they found it impossible to look beyond the immediate conflict and make choices less destructive of the family. Is this simply not possible when overwhelmed by the belief that *Mother always loved you best?*

Before the older daughter left town, she phoned me again. The reconciliation she sought had been refused. I did not ask whether she looked back on their earlier bitter contest with regret, but I know the answer.

A Protocol Is Needed

My friend's son is divorcing, ending a twenty-five-year marriage. Although sad, my friend doesn't question the decision. He sensed from the sidelines that neither partner had been happy for some time, and he was aware of their sincere efforts to work things out.

He and his daughter-in-law had come to know each other well in recent years, drawn together as she lovingly helped to care for his wife during her final illness. Often she was on call to be present when he had to be away, and upon his return, they would talk over coffee, engaged in ever more meaningful conversations evoked by the impending loss of his life partner and his own advancing years. His wife as well had come to think of their daughter-in-law as a daughter of her own, and a deepening friendship had grown between them. He was sure that despite the marital rift, his daughter-in-law would remain a cherished member of his family.

So throughout the difficult months of the couple's estrangement and then their separation, my friend was determined to preserve good relations not only with his son but also with his son's soon to be former wife. She continued to join him for occasional meals and from time to time they spoke by phone, skirting the subject of the marriage that was ending. She even talked with him about others with whom she was developing new connections.

One evening when he was at a concert, soon after the divorcing couple entered the legal arena, he encountered his daughter-in-law's parents. They were cool to him and hastened their departure. It was upsetting but understandable, he thought, and shrugged it off. He wouldn't even bring it up. At least his relationship with his daughter-in-law would not change. But, of course, it had already changed.

As the legal process escalated, her hurt and anger toward his son rose. Her feeling that she was the one more aggrieved slowly seeped into every conversation and email. At first she would make only a nuanced negative remark. But soon she spoke more unguardedly of his son's failings. Lawyer involvement increased and settlement talks faltered. My friend made no response, staying silent or attempting to change the subject. He thought the communication boundaries were clear, but they continued to erode. No longer able to be empathic in the face of her repeated accusations, their contact ended.

When he spoke of his dilemma to others, many responded quickly and easily, "Blood is thicker than water." He remained unwilling to be judgmental, wise enough to know that no one but the marriage partners themselves could speak of the realities and that even their perceptions would surely differ.

"I love them both dearly," he lamented, "but I've lost the close bond I so valued with my daughter-in-law."

I didn't think it had to stay lost in the long term, so I offered stories of others I've known, myself included, who mended similar relationships once the most painful time of the marital collapse and its aftermath had passed. For one, I renewed my connection with my son's former wife. Although I had to acknowledge that the nature of that connection had changed, it was still loving and even intimate at times. But other doors would always remain closed.

So many important attachments are lost to both parties when the terrible angst of divorce seems to call for taking sides. Need they be? Perhaps not. Extended family members and common friends need a protocol and an agreed-upon time out. Necessary boundaries should be made clear and be respected, to protect against hurtful expressions of disloyalty toward one or the other and to avoid a permanent breach. In an ideal world, friends and extended family would make communication boundaries explicit, even written in a thoughtful note expressing sadness but a hoped-for future. But perhaps more than anything, we need to have realistic expectations of the significant healing time required for friendship to win out over recrimination and the pain of loss.

Significant Memories

Still pondering the idea of writing a book, I look for expert advice, and what I find goes beyond my immediate quest.

The agent Susan Rabiner asks prospective authors of serious nonfiction this question: "Why is your work important?" In her view a book must present an argument, not simply report research conclusions, or tell a story.*

If writers cannot readily answer this question, she urges us to recall events of our youth that forecast the adult--- memories of those times that ignited the passion for what we are writing about now. Recapturing those memories, she proposes, will define what motivates us today and provide the argument for writing the book.

And, I wonder, for life? If important transitions lie ahead, as we move from one role to another---a new job, retirement, a book--- what direction makes sense?

I asked a friend of mine what childhood memories pointed to his future outcomes.

"My parents always stressed," he said, "that I must do the right, the just thing. If a merchant ever gave me back too much change, no question, I had to return it."

"Then in the fifth grade, the teacher accused a girl in my class, somewhat of an outsider, of a bad act. I knew she had not committed it. With self-righteousness only a fifth grader could muster, I approached the teacher's desk and asked, 'Miss Jones, do you believe in the Ten Commandments?' She said: 'Of course,' so I went on, 'Do you know the one about not bearing false witness?'

"That night I told my mother about the encounter. She was mortified and promptly called the teacher to offer an apology for my behavior. 'Oh, but he was absolutely right,' was the teacher's surprising response."

The story became a family classic.

The player in this drama, a man in his early seventies, grew up in a small town, was a leader, and excelled in school. As we talked, he was able to bring forth more early memories of encouraging others, and himself, to do the "right thing", to meet his need for justice.

After college he entered a major urban law school and on graduation was hired by a prestigious firm. Assigned work crafting and closing on contracts for corporate mergers and acquisitions, he found he had neither enthusiasm nor competence for these tasks. When a senior partner proposed he take on a pro bono project helping organize an inner-city heath clinic, he eagerly accepted and was immediately fully engaged with the people, doctors and nurses, and their mission.

Soon afterward he left the lucrative law firm job. For many of the years that followed, he developed programs to provide legal representation for the disadvantaged, reflecting his zeal for righting wrongs.

I'm learning about myself in posing this question to my friends. As they bring to mind how certain early events shaped their essence, their destinations, I do so as well. I'd never before thought of using important memories in this way, to analyze the "argument" for what is being written, and to inform the future.

(*Thinking Like Your Editor: How to Write Great Serious Non-Fiction)

A Father's Day Wish

A small porcelain bird sits on a shelf in my bedroom. If I glance away from reading the morning paper or when I check the illuminated dial of my clock, it is always in view. It's not something I would have purchased for myself---too cute, too sentimental. But it was a gift from my father.

He brought it to my home over fifty years ago when he traveled to my city on business, a rare visit unaccompanied by my mother. He'd probably purchased it at an airport kiosk. It was the only present I, as an adult, ever received from him that hadn't been handed to me, and likely chosen, by my mother.

After our marriage, Len and I lived quite some distance from both sets of parents. We visited them several times a year, and in that pre-Internet era wrote often and had weekly long-distance phone conversations. The letters I received were in my mother's hand and she did most of the talking on the phone, with my father listening on an extension. When my parents were together, it was my mother who filled the air with her presence.

My father died in 1977. I regret not having sought to know him better after leaving home at seventeen for college. Three years later, while we were still at school, Len and I married, so I never again spent an extended period of time alone with him. He was a kind, quiet, and reserved man who readily answered questions about his views on politics or world affairs. But during our family visits, even those conversations were often interrupted by one of my youngsters or when my mother raised a practical concern of the moment.

Thinking back, I knew little about the feelings hidden behind this man's gentle smile. He immigrated to this country as a teenager, struggled to get a foothold, then lost virtually everything after the 1929 crash and had to start over. He left our house early every morning before I was up and about and rode the Grand Central Railroad into New York City, worked long hours to rebuild his family's security, then usually returned well after dinner.

My husband's experience with his parents was not too different. He had a vibrant mother who held the family together at home, while his father commuted to long and arduous workdays in Chicago, returned home weary and often wordlessly retreated into a world of music, his piano.

Born of this past, many years ago Len and I realized that we wanted our adult children to really come to know their father, another quiet man, in ways we both had missed. So when we phoned our grown kids, we did not share the conversation. One of us would talk and then hand off the phone to the other. I, the more verbal parent, did not eclipse the other.

And Len went a step further. He took our older grown-up son on an extended canoe trip into the Canadian wilderness. After our second son reached adulthood, they flew together in Len's small plane to revisit the remote western towns where the family had spent summers many years before. Later, with our fifteen-year-old daughter, he flew off to Alaska for a camping adventure neither would ever forget.

At least once a year we visited our adult children separately, traveling alone to their distant homes. Even without witnessing the quality of their interaction when I wasn't there, I knew my absence made their connection with him more significant. I, in turn, enjoyed being with them on my own.

Len wept bitterly at his father's funeral for what never had been.

And I wish I'd been wise enough, so many years ago, to be more aware of what I was missing.

Troubling Fantasies

I've experienced the suicide of two friends, as adults. Both came as a shock, and sometimes as betrayals, and it remains to contemplate the desperate sadness that must have driven them to the act. But in the end I came to accept that these two friends had made well-considered, mature decisions.

On learning of a recent teenage suicide, however, I can almost hear the sharp intake of breath I share with others. I can never accept that the young take this path.

It was about thirty years ago, our family court was rocked by two teenage suicides, one following the other by only months, their parents locked in *War of the Roses* combat. Shocked and saddened, a colleague of mine was galvanized to action. Our collective sorrow led us to seek greater understanding about children experiencing traumatic times. We yearned for knowledge that would draw us back from hell and into the light.

The result: An expert from out of town was invited to come and steer us in some new directions. Neil Kalter, a research psychologist and author of *Growing Up with Divorce*, addressed a large group of lawyers, mental health professionals and virtually all of the court personnel, judges, magistrates and parenting specialists. Some things he said that day, I continued to repeat to all parents I meet with, usually on the very first day of mediation.

He said, "All children of divorce experience two fantasies."

I remember being surprised that this well regarded social scientist was willing to be so universal in his approach.

Divorcing parents eventually separate, Kalter continued, by way of explanation. Children who have only experienced a home with both father and mother present, fantasize that if one parent can leave, what's to keep the other parent from leaving? The fear imagined is of complete abandonment. That is their first fantasy.

Kalter suggested parents be urged to reassure their kids, who rarely speak of this fear, that despite their separation, both parents will always be there for them. And these encouraging words should not be spoken only once, but repeated often during the difficult early days and beyond. Every time I think about this and mention it to others, I'm surprised anew that it was not more obvious to me before that day, but it was not.

The second fantasy Kalter described was far less easy for me to understand. "Children of divorce blame themselves for the divorce." I remember wondering how or why this could be? Perhaps, I thought, it might be true of adolescents, acting out in negative ways as they push away from childhood, but otherwise it made little sense. Well, I've become a believer, for as I tell parents about this, they often shake their heads in sad acknowledgment.

The father of a seven-year-old just recently told me he overheard his son tell a playmate, "If only I had done my homework, my parents would not have split."

It would almost be funny if it were not so sad.

Permission Granted

Have you ever called upon a friend or loved one to talk over a decision you were considering, only to later realize you were actually seeking permission to take a step that was out of step with what others may have expected of you? Were you reluctant to disappoint or even shock those you hold dear? If so, consider this a benefit of true friendship, which can also be the reward of consultation with a trusted adviser.

Here is what brought these thoughts to mind:

The woman with whom I was having lunch was a nurse, specially trained as a geriatric care manager. I sought her out to talk about her work and she shared this view: "We are so conditioned by the 'shoulds' and 'oughts' of the culture, religion and the times in which we were raised, that sometimes we need to be given permission by another to make the wise rational choices to best care for ourselves and our loved ones."

She told me about her experience with her eighty-eight year old father who was hospitalized for over two weeks and not expected to survive, but he did. His clear instructions were, "If this happens to me again, no more heroics, too much pain and too much expense. Just let me go."

She was quick to respond and reassure, "But I'm not ready to let you go."

Her father's answer: "This is not your decision to make."

She realized he was not only stating his wishes but also giving her permission to carry them out.

My naïve question about her father, "But didn't he have a living will?" He did. But her professional experience taught her that despite properly executed living wills, when confronted with end of life decisions, the designated decision maker is frequently unable to act in accord with the legal document, is immobilized. Permission must still be granted.

Another example: A sixty year old woman, the sole caretaker for her eighty-two year old mother, entered the care manager's office saying, "I hate my mother."

Despite a childhood endured with an alcoholic and abusive parent, and a troubled distant relationship with her as an adult, when her mother could no longer live independently, the daughter felt she had no option but to provide care in her home. Both were miserable. The advice given: "The obligation to honor a parent presumes having been honored, as a child and as an adult." Permission was granted and the mother was moved to a nursing home.

And another example offered by the care manager: She had attended a conference for fellow professionals who were addressed by a renowned Rabbi educator. He suggested it was time to reconsider the concept of adultery. His shocked audience was then told of a seventy-two year old man whose wife, two years earlier, had suffered a major stroke that left her seriously impaired, both physically and mentally, and was now resident in a nursing home. He sought and found the companionship of another woman, but so far had denied himself the fullness of the relationship he desired. Permission was granted.

The "shoulds" and "oughts" of life are programmed into our DNA, or so it seems. There are times when the greatest gift a friend or counselor can bestow is to sanction our setting aside restrictions and obligations we have internalized, but which no longer make sense.

Even with the wisdom of years, permission must still be granted.

So, to my dear children: "If and when the time arrives when I am no longer able to care for myself, utilize my long-term care insurance to keep me in my home or to house me in a decent facility, not in your home. If you don't live nearby, frequent emails and only occasional visits will be just fine. If you are close by, once a week will do. And should I no longer recognize you or treat you lovingly, just check on me once in a while." Permission granted.

A Promise Not Kept

Newspaper wedding announcements catch my eye, especially those that tell a romantic tale of how the loving relationship evolved to commitment. I don't even read them with a cynical eye, despite my work with those whose bonds are unraveling. But I do wonder if those who preside over marriage rituals today, or the wedding partners themselves, make the same "until death do us part" promise to each other, as in days gone by?

Isn't it fair to say that every promise we make to another is conditioned on underlying, often unspoken, assumptions? Even marriage vows. And if the early life experiences of the two partners have generated different, undisclosed, and perhaps even unrecognized assumptions, then what?

A recent conversation with mediation clients sparked this old memory: As a very young child, I often woke early on Sunday mornings to a silent house, my older brothers still asleep. I'd leave my bed and wander to the door of my parents' room where I would settle down on the floor, waiting until I sensed the time was right to knock and join them under the covers. Sitting there, I listened to their murmurings. Although unable to detect recognizable words, I could discern the voice of one and then the other, and I imagined them close to each other, warm and cozy, talking things over.

Many years later, I married a man of Norwegian heritage, in whose childhood home talk was sparse. He grew up well accustomed to silence. It's hardly any wonder that the early years of our marriage brought disappointment for me in the talking realm, and frustration for Len at my persistent yearning for a greater sharing of feelings. But over time our relationship evolved, with some help from the "talking cure", a skilled therapist. And now one of my fondest memories is of our Sunday mornings. Both early risers, once our oldest was in his teens, we left our two younger kids asleep in his charge, and we shared a nearby cozy restaurant nook for a leisurely breakfast. We maintained the practice even after our nest was empty. We talked of the week past and that ahead, or any worry either of us needed to air. The talk was not always happy, I suppose, but now the memory is golden.

Recently, a divorcing pair found their way to my office. Neither spouse had been unfaithful, and they had had no violent arguments. But they lived like brother and sister, with a pervasive polite coolness. After a year of counseling, sometimes together, sometimes alone, the husband was adamant that the vows they spoke when they married bound them to soldier on and maintain the marriage. The wife reached an opposite conclusion.

For complex reasons unique to each couple contemplating this tortuous decision, the marital promises they made, premised on assumptions about love, passion, understanding, and acceptance, are sometimes realized, and sometimes not. Those couples who are willing to do the hard work of unearthing hidden expectations may successfully reach new understandings and come to honor rather than disparage or ignore each other's differences.

This husband was determined to maintain the status quo, however barren. The wife carefully considered her response. "Is that really the loving thing to do?" she asked. "In terms of others, even if not myself, would I be doing a good thing to stay in the marriage? Does it help or hurt us, or our children? I don't want us to model for them that this is what a marriage should be. We may or may not find new loving relationships, but I want them to know that it is something that both of their parents deserve, and that one day they will as well."

Often what we witness in our homes as children is what we come to expect, or consciously decide to reject, in our adult lives. Some who grew up witnessing violence, or were plagued by pervasive parental disapproval, struggle to avoid replicating these ways for their own families and succeed. But many other times the cycle of abuse is perpetuated. What about a determination to perpetuate a cycle of love?

Who Else Is in Bed?

Many moons ago, a clever psychologist observed that there are always six people in every marriage bed: the husband, the wife and both sets of parents. A recent experience reminded me that we never travel down the path to any decision truly alone.

A young divorcing couple were planning their lives as parents when no longer married, slowly working their way through all of the traumas and difficult choices, aware and worried about their lives ahead without love and with financial hardship. Their very young child seemed to be adapting to the sea change in their lives with greater ease than either of them.

Although divided about many things, from the outset of mediation they were completely in sync about their goals for their child and even about promoting each other's chances for future well-being. Splitting up their accumulated assets was easy. Coping with their high mortgage payments was less so. But the husband, a medical researcher, was willing to contribute the lion's share of his income to finance the marital residence for two years for the sake of stability, and thereby also avoid a fire sale in a weak housing market. And as their daughter was so young, he readily agreed that his wife should not seek a job until their child was school age. He would rent a small apartment nearby and live frugally. The chips were all falling into place.

And then they weren't.

His lawyer strongly objected to the level of support he proposed to contribute for the next two years, saying, "No court would ever make you pay so much. She's bleeding you dry. She needs to get a job and help with the mortgage or else sell the house. I can't let you do this."

On their return to mediation he announced he had changed his mind, and his wife was soon in tears. He asked to speak with me alone.

"It isn't just my lawyer," he told me, "although she says I'm being a fool. It's everyone else too. Since I'm the one who's leaving, I'm made out to be the bad guy. But trust me, we've both been miserable for a long time. My friends, and even my parents, say I'm crazy, letting my guilt get ahead of my reason. I want her to keep the house, and be a full-time mom, but maybe it's just not possible."

His use of the word *maybe* told me about the pull between where his heart led him and the dictates of his lawyer, and about his need to seem forceful in the eyes of those in his own camp. These bystanders, who likely saw themselves as fulfilling their role as advocates and as loyal supporters, fueled an anger and resentment he'd not previously expressed.

Ironically, if they sold the house now, likely at a loss, it might well leave them less financially secure. Could his wife, a graphic artist, find a job earning enough to even meet the cost of their child's day care? And most important, what would happen to the ease that had evolved as he and his wife related as parents?

When I raised these questions, he nodded his understanding but said only that he needed more time to think it over.

Would he be strong enough to withstand the judgment of others, who portrayed him as impotent and his wife as domineering?

His compatriots, invisible contributors to the decisions he faced when negotiating in my office, were sabotaging his better judgment. A group decision was being made. Could he pull himself away and stand alone?

His wife was out of the marriage bed, but many others had climbed in.

Fathers, Past and Present

It's surely true for all of us: our personal past informs our professional present.

The father seated in my office weeps without shame. He and his wife have not yet told their eleven-year-old daughter that their marriage is ending. For both of them, it looms as a painful task, but he is the parent who feels most at risk of losing or diminishing the precious connection to this child. Although he has been much more involved in raising her than fathers were in years past, his work commitments meant that his wife assumed the primary parenting role.

Will he continue to have a secure place in his daughter's life when living on his own and no longer with her for part of every day? He fears he will not. I empathize and want to reassure him, but how?

I have few childhood memories of my own father, except at Sunday dinners, for he was usually absent as I was growing up. To keep bread on the table during the Depression, he left home before I awoke and returned after dark. Then, just as our financial fortunes began to ease, came the horrors of the Holocaust, World War II, my older brother's entry into the army, and the detonation of atomic bombs. These events commanded my family's attention during my teen years. Just after the war ended, I left home for college, returning only for brief visits.

But one personal memory remains vivid. When I was eleven years old, I cut my own hair, snipping off long locks to create bangs. My mother did not hide her utter dismay. When my father came home, she brought him to view the damage. But even in the face of my his wife's frowning disapproval, he said, "I like it very much. She's very pretty."

My spirits soared. It was an important moment for me, still remembered so many decades later.

My perhaps idealized memory of my father is of a quiet, kind man, always with a newspaper in hand, who seemed pleased whenever he

saw me. I grew up believing he loved and approved of me uncondi-
tionally. I did not fully appreciate this gift until much later in life,
when a close friend told me her abiding memory was of her father's
relentless disapproval.

I told my sorrowful client this story in a private moment when next
we met, and I suggested that his daughter would never forget the important kindnesses he showed her in the past and that he would still
show her in the future. Though no longer a constant presence in her
life, there would now be moments that just the two of them would
share. Some will be memorable. He smiled but retreated into silence.

The other father I have known well is the man I married. Len
strove to be a father like my own, and mostly he was until he wasn't.
In the early 1970s, as the Vietnam War raged, conversations at our
dinner table, and on the university campus where he taught, roiled
with dissent. The sexual revolution was in full swing just as our teenagers came of age. As parents, we sought to adjust to the swiftly
changing times, but we were in turmoil, trying to understand but still
hold to standards we thought sound.

One day Len came home and found one of our sons upstairs with a
girlfriend. In anger he told him it must never happen again or he
would have to leave. It was our house, so our rules applied. I silently
acquiesced to his edict, agreeing with his reasons but less sure about
the threat and alert to the rage in which he made his quick decision,
knowing some but not all of its sources.

Defiant, our son moved to a tiny apartment (guess who paid the
rent?) until he left for college some months later. But as children grow
to maturity, they learn to see their parents in the context of their times
and unique personal history. In the years that followed, both father
and son apologized, and the relationship became relaxed and loving
once again. I shared this story with my sorrowful client as well: We
can repair our missteps.

And what is the message from fathers today? Anything goes, just
stay safe?

Conflicted

A m I the only parent of grown children who is conflicted about their visits? Two live far off, the other several hours away. They lead busy complicated lives, so they don't come often. They would come more frequently if I asked them to, but I do not ask. It is our email, text, and phone connection that is constant and comforting.

But on special days, I happily anticipate their arrival, and it is wonderful to see them, to hold them close. So why, two days later as they are packing to leave, am I relieved to have them on their way? And why, after they are gone, am I lonelier and more troubled than I was before they came?

My older son came last weekend accompanied by a loving partner. The morning after our joyous coming together, my son, his wife, and I sit at breakfast and make plans for a movie and dinner out. We foresee a frolic, an escape, but from what?

On our return home, we call my son's far-away sister, and the conversation becomes private as he carries the phone off to a corner of the room. I'm reassured by their intimacy, knowing they will have each other to rely on when I can no longer protect them should troubles arise. Of course, this thought is absurd, for I can't protect them now. But shouldn't I, the mother? Or have the tables already turned?

The lighthearted day ends with ice cream. But the next morning, my son's face looks downcast, although no one besides me appears to take notice. I ask if he slept well, and he tells me he did not. Were there disturbing interactions of which I'm unaware? Was some old family tension intruding on our perfect gathering, showing it to be make-believe? Perhaps I should ask, but I do not.

Then he rises from the breakfast table and moves to stand behind the woman with whom he is rebuilding a house and a life. He gently kneads the tense muscles of her neck and shoulders. The message is clear: We are in this together. I'm here for you, to pleasure you, to work with you, a constant presence in your life.

I am both relieved and pained, for I remember that touch, so often received from my lost loved husband. My throat tightens. They know well how I miss him. They miss him too, but do not speak of him. Do they think it would make me sad? It would not.

Lingering over coffee, laptops at fingertips, concerns arise of approaching bad weather, and the leave-taking is hastened. Smiling departures are made, with hugs and promises of future visits.

Then my rooms are empty. I go about the satisfying task of returning seldom-used items to their well-ordered places. Glad to be alone, I try to push concern aside, and name it as theirs, no longer mine. But it doesn't work. What has triggered my melancholy? An old family trouble come back to life? Was it something I did or failed to do? Should I have probed, asked more questions? Or am I misreading the signs? If I had not glimpsed that look of sadness, would I now be at ease? The thought that follows: A parent should be able to restore a child's wellbeing. Twisted thinking. He is not a child, and for me to probe, uninvited, would be to meddle. How can I help? I cannot. I should not? I'm conflicted.

There are so many emotional undercurrents when families reconnect. For us, they usually remain unspoken when we are together, to be sorted out when we return to our separate lives. Is this a failing? Then I recall the boundaries that my husband and I maintained with our own parents, as we worked out whatever difficulty each or both of us faced. That felt right. Independent. Mature.

I will get on with managing my own life. They will manage theirs. My son is a grown man with a loving partner. I need to let go, and I will.

Tomorrow, or the next day.

CHAPTER FOUR

ANGER AND BLAME

Verbal Jujitsu

If you believe that it's important for intimate partners to work through conflicts as they arise, it is probably counter-intuitive to be told that sometimes conflict avoidance may be the better course. But such can be the case when one partner is faced with words meant to intimidate. I develop this premise here in the context of a divorce, but believe it holds true in any personal negotiation.

The story: The timbre of my caller's voice conveyed the intensity of his emotional state. Not bothering with any opening pleasantries, he curtly told me he was calling to inquire about mediation only at his wife's insistence. For a few moments, he allowed me to describe the process, but he soon interrupted to express his skepticism. His wife, he told me, was inflexible about the issue most important to him. "I'll consider mediation," he concluded, "only if she agrees in advance that she'll share time with our children equally. Otherwise I'm filing for sole custody."

I was reasonably sure that this warning was born of his anxiety that divorce would seriously diminish his precious connection with his children. So while I empathized with his concern, I gently urged him not to throw down the gauntlet: "Threats beget threats--- and often lengthy litigation."

Silence at first. Then he told me that he and his wife had been attempting to negotiate terms on their own. They had started out talking in a relaxed way, for their past relationship had been a respectful one. But their marriage bond was now frayed, so even the tone in which one of them said something, or made a proposal, could lead to frustration or even trigger anger. Their discussion would then escalate into dueling ultimatums.

Can the effort to intimidate just be ignored? It rarely is, but actually that may be the wisest course: to step aside without striking back. Verbal jujitsu.

Most threats are born of fear, and it is the fear that needs to be explored and understood rather than the menacing words. But too often the fight-or-flight response takes over, precluding rational discourse.

In the divorce context, verbal threats are legion, as in *I'll sue for custody before I ever accept one minute less than equal time with the children.* Or: *I'll go to jail before I pay a dime of alimony, when you're the one who wants this.* Or: *I'll disclose the pornography I found on your computer if you fight me on this point.*

If a partner's sincere goal is to move the other toward agreement---which it almost always is---then to counter in kind may well destroy the chance of settlement. An opposing response made in the heat of the moment will only make it more difficult for the speaker to later retreat. Both parties need to buy time to cool down.

There are other options.

If sufficient calm prevails, a mediator or dispassionate mutual friend can meet with each party privately to discuss the possible or likely consequences of the threatened action. That can be an important reality check.

Even more helpful is for the third party to ask the partner who issued the challenge why they feel so strongly about the issue. Such a discussion (often a tearful interlude) can give rise to a catharsis.

But if the amount of tension already generated is so great as to preclude either person from being able to listen to the other with understanding, an equally useful tactic is to move on to a discussion of a completely unrelated topic, allowing passions to cool. Sidestep the issue. Verbal jujitsu.

As the mediator, this is the choice I usually make if the parties will accept the diversion. And it is a choice individuals can make on their own, without announcement. The passage of time will likely allow for a return to reason, especially if both partners are able to acknowledge the fear underlying the threat, usually of some loss or perceived loss, and then address it. At such times, taking a moment to express sincere compassion can cause incredible shifts in position.

It often behooves the party who was threatened to recognize that ignoring the threat will allow the other to save face---and so is their own best choice. Continue to ignore the threat, and certainly refrain from repeating it to allies on the sidelines. Simply step aside from the menacing words so that both parties can refocus on what they hope to achieve for the long term. Verbal jujitsu.

Anger Revisited

As the scientific study of anger evolved, I failed to keep up. Until very recently I continued to believe that suppressing this emotion leads to high blood pressure and depression, and that the healthier path was to seek outlets, even physical release, for one's anger. Here is how my new understanding unfolded:

A husband and wife entered mediation hoping to maintain a friendly relationship as parents, and their conversation in my presence was moderate, if guarded. Privately, to me, each described unhappy years as they drifted apart, and each blamed the other for the failure of the marriage. But our work was proceeding well.

Then one day the husband forwarded to me an email to his lawyer instructing him, in clipped abrupt language, to inform his wife's counsel that he had cancelled the insurance on her car. I called him to discuss his decision. Sounding tense, he reminded me of his wife's reluctance to seek employment. "I have to carry more than my share of the load," he said. "I've had it!"

During a phone call the night before, he told me, something his wife had said sparked his resentment, and he gave full force and voice to his anger. The end result: the next morning he decided to cancel her insurance.

"I get it," I said. "Venting provided some release, but reconsider the cancellation. You two are well on the way to completing your entire agreement. Will your move provoke a counter move and derail the process? Think it over. You play golf. Get out there and whack a bucket of balls."

He agreed, and I felt wise. But apparently I was not.

Coincident with these events, I happened to be reading a fascinating 2007 book by two prominent social psychologists, *Mistakes Were Made (but not by me): Why We Justify Foolish Beliefs, Bad Decisions, and Hurtful Acts*. Carol Tavris and Elliot Aronson argue that the commonly held belief that expressing anger results in a healthy catharsis and reduced blood pressure is dead wrong. The findings of the experiments that the authors cite establish that those who give full sway to their anger (i.e. shouting at a family member when provoked, or hitting a punching bag while imagining the source of your anger) get angrier, not less angry. Their conclusion: "aggression begets self-justification, which begets more aggression."

Following an angry outburst, the mechanism of self-justification takes over, in order that we can continue to see ourselves as good people, worthy of self-esteem. Once we mitigate or excuse our own behavior, our predictable next step is to place blame on the "other", which in a moment of increased aggressive feelings often leads to taking revenge (i.e. canceling the insurance).

Mental health professionals distinguish between suppressed and repressed anger. Suppression is perfectly fine if we do it for good reason (i.e. to avoid losing a job), while repressing our awareness of anger, and its source, can lead to trouble.

So, I called my client back and described my newly gained insight, "I think it's a good thing to recognize and even taste your anger," I said, "and do your best to understand the source. But scratch the golf ball plan. Try a hot fudge sundae instead."

He decided not to cancel the insurance.

Blame and Guilt

"I feel terrible," she said. "You've ruined my life!"

As she sobbed, her husband, silent, sat at the other end of my long office couch, awash in guilt. He had made the final decision to divorce, but his compassion for his wife was sincere. I wanted to somehow calm and comfort them both, to reassure him by saying that relationships rarely fail for simple one-sided reasons, and assure her that I empathized with her misery. But I said nothing.

In a few moments her tears lessened and she regained self-control. She apologized to me for her outburst. "No need," I said.

The blaming was over, for now. We returned to talk about their budgets and how the family could best share their joint income.

Nine months of marital counseling had ended just weeks before they began mediation. Did she really believe that she had no part to play as they drifted apart and moved into separate bedrooms? At times it seemed so. But she was mature enough to hold on to their determination to end things as amicably as possible and preserve as much stability as they could for their children.

Husbands and wives, all partners, inevitably both delight and disappoint each other. Delight, is easy, but disappointment too often gives rise to both blame and guilt.

The tearful scene in my office brings to mind the guilt I felt for many years for having failed Len. From the beginning, he and I talked through and jointly made important decisions. Then as our years together multiplied, we often wordlessly simply accommodated to the other's wishes, knowing which particular outcome mattered most to each of us. At least, that's the way I now choose to remember it.

It usually worked well, but there was an exception. Len yearned to live near water, by the sea or a large lake. Either would do, so long as he could experience its wonders and the tranquility that vast waters offered him. And, of course, the fishing potential!

But with his new PhD, a wife and young children in hand, life took us to his job in land-locked southern Ohio, at a time when college teaching posts were hard to come by. Law school followed for me, and some years later my growing successful practice became another anchor. He gloried in his summer teaching work in the Rocky Mountains, where clear roiling trout streams filled his every spare hour. But in the grayness of Midwestern winters, he yearned to move and often seemed sad. Witnessing this, not sharing his wish to leave, I avoided addressing his apparent unhappiness. My guilt feelings were at times intense.

But then a conversation with a wise psychologist friend caused me to shift mental gears. She suggested that as adults we are responsible to make those decisions that are important to our own well-being. Of course. Len could have developed a specific plan to move and proposed it. But he made no serious search for other job options, in effect choosing to foster my career over his own enjoyment of water.

Still, he was not passive. He learned to fly, and with the help of my additional income, he bought a small plane. Some time later he opted for early retirement and for over fourteen years he flew off with like-minded students and friends to wherever the geology was exciting and the fish were biting, exploring the Great Lakes, the national parks, and Alaska. We each had our cake.

In some divorcing couples, parties maintain that in an effort to avoid conflict, they chose to abdicate the decider role. Then when conflict takes center stage, they look back and resent having lost their authenticity, the power to direct their own life, wishing they had taken other paths. But with certain exceptions---those coming from families subjected to violence and single parents of young children---adults are responsible for designing their own destiny.

The blame game is neither fair nor in the long run satisfying. Nor is the guilt.

The Evil Twin

S he called to apologize and left me this message: *Forgive my miserable behavior. It was my evil twin, Skippy, talking.*

I smiled, remembering a bit of wisdom often spoken by my husband: "No one ever sees themselves as evil."

Earlier that day Jenny, a mediation client, had unleashed angry accusations at her partner. Now, on reflection, she attributed them to her imaginary evil twin, Skippy.

Jenny and Bruce had lived together for ten years, unmarried. Then, sadly but amiably, they decided to go their separate ways. Both had previously been divorced and when they first came together and blended their families, they had been raising teenagers. Now they'd come to mediation to design an agreement for an equitable parting.

Their decisions had few legal ramifications---although many couples live together unmarried today, in most states few laws govern their separations. They spoke of honoring their past contributions to their life together, and both said they hoped to maintain the close parental relationships each had formed with the other's children, now grown.

Not surprisingly, as their negotiation began, they soon discovered they had begun mediation with different expectations. Although they shared the goal of seeking a fair outcome, each defined "fair" according to standards they did not share.

When they first got together, both had been salaried employees. Bruce, with a far greater income, paid the mortgage and most of the day-to-day household expenses. Jenny then started her own business, which Bruce subsidized with a generous loan of $50,000. Over time her business became a consuming passion, and she fully repaid his loan. Now her earnings were significantly greater than his. She had hired six employees and outsiders were making overtures to purchase the company.

When her evil twin, Skippy, intervened in the discussion, it was just after Bruce expressed his belief that he should share in the present value of, or receive an ownership interest in, Jenny's business. His emotional support, financial investment, and advice, he maintained, had been crucial to her success.

Shocked by this request, Jenny disparaged the worth of his contribution. Their discussion became heated, and Jenny grew accusatory. In essence:

Jenny: "This is sheer greed on your part!"

Bruce: "But for me, you would never have made it."

And on and on. They left my office angry and upset.

Later, when I got her "Skippy" message and returned her call, she was calmer and again expressed regret. I asked if she could consider that Bruce did not speak as a greedy evildoer but from good intentions, even if from her perspective, mistaken? Could she quell her anxiety about the perceived assault on her venture, her very independence, long enough to hear him?

She told me she was aware that if they had married, Bruce would have been legally entitled to share in the value of her business. So, I posed: "Is that a public policy worth taking into account, even if you are not legally bound to do so? And most important, what actions would best meet your shared long-term goal of continued family friendships?"

Accepting the reality that no one perceives themselves as evil calls for an important shift in perspective, the offer of a measure of respect for the other's point of view. While this won't present immediate solutions, it makes possible the development of settlement options.

If Skippy can be kept at bay.

The Allure of Self-Justification

Inadvertently, or thoughtlessly, I so angered a lawyer colleague that she ended our phone conversation by abruptly hanging up.

Dazed and unbelieving, still holding the dark screen of my phone in hand, I tried to replay the back-and-forth talk. But except for a phrase or two, at that moment I could not. Something she said had evoked my laughter, which she took as a lack of respect for her, and she said so. Then despite my quick brief apology, she said a firm goodbye and broke the connection.

I had called her with a specific goal in mind. She'd given advice to one of my mediation clients, and I wanted to change her thinking. I considered my position so well reasoned that this hardly seemed a daunting task. But it was. She found no merit in my perspective and instead presented her own. I then refuted her thinking, as she did mine. Neither of us asked thoughtful questions of the other, only issued critiques. Then I laughed, and she abruptly ended the call.

After a few moments, I turned to other tasks, unsuccessfully. I couldn't remember another time when someone's anger had caused them to hang up on me. So I called a friend who I knew would lend her support and humor to my rant and help me analyze what had just taken place. She was indeed reassuring, concluding that the other's angry manner was wholly uncalled for and urged me to simply disregard it. That was calming, for a time. I turned to my evening's planned diversions and put the matter out of mind.

But the morning light brought continued unease I could not put aside.

Why was so much tension injected into a call that began with a friendly exchange, both of us expressing appreciation for our renewed contact? As we talked, the difference in our viewpoints expanded. We became adversaries. Did either of us seriously listen to what the other had to say, really try to understand? I had to acknowledge that I had not. If I had, would she have done the same?

I'd allowed the consultation to seek options for resolution of an issue to evolve into a reckless debate. I began to see clearly how I had succumbed to the allure of self-justification, and to blaming the other when something goes awry.

At mid-morning, I emailed her a sincere apology for my role in the donnybrook, reaffirmed my respect for her, and suggested we get together for lunch, for a more relaxed exchange.

Some hours later she replied: "Apology accepted. . . having an extremely rushed week with complications . . . I will call you to schedule lunch. Thanks for your message."

Here's what I know: We see the issues under discussion very differently, and perhaps do not even share the same values on these points. But even if we cannot agree, we can certainly come to better understand and respect the other's viewpoint. Next time I will really listen and probe for understanding. Perhaps she will mirror my approach, or perhaps not.

We just might develop some creative solutions. And even if we don't, I'll be at ease.

What's the Payoff?

D ear M and D:
    Were you as relieved as I was when you left my office? Witnessing the animosity, blame and disrespect with which you assault each other leaves me both amazed and dismayed. Did you feel equally disheartened? Or perhaps you welcomed having a safe haven in which to publicly expose your frustration and anger. You test both my skill and my endurance. Can I possibly help you resolve your issues?

From time to time I'm faced with warring parents, long divorced like you, who've never given up the fight. For them I have only questions, no answers.

You tell me you recognize that your daughters are troubled, and you both acknowledge that in light of your open conflict, this is hardly surprising. Child specialists teach that children internalize the character, the essence, of both parents, and to the extent one parent denigrates the other, the child's self-esteem is diminished. You both bear witness to the damage being done.

After you left, I wondered: Was yours a studied performance, or were you really out of control? Were you acting out dissatisfaction in your individual lives? Were you howling at the moon, rather than at each other? Or were you following an old childhood script, never having learned another? It was surely a passionate dance I witnessed, alternately one of you leading, the other in pursuit.

A psychiatrist friend with whom I shared these questions wondered about you: "What's the payoff? What benefits are these parents each receiving from their persistent warfare?" He says we revert to those ways that are personally satisfying: to relieve stress, to set right some imbalance, or perhaps to enjoy the comfort of behavior consistent with our early experience, even if it is hurtful. Likely unseen by another, he noted, these rewards support the pattern of actions that repeat and repeat.

I know I see only the surface of your relationship, and I don't have the analytical skill to draw conclusions. But really, what's the payoff? Does keeping your conflict alive serve you in some important way? Perhaps even allow you to remain connected?

Am I wrong, or in the midst of your refusal to give even an inch in the direction of the other, did I glimpse in some offhand comments a hint that there are times, when out of view, you relate with a measure of civility and respect? Or is this wishful thinking on my part? Might you as parents be able to tap some remnant of feeling to come to the rescue of your daughters?

When you left my office, did you feel better or worse?

In both of you, I recognize intelligence and love for your children, a genuine concern for their safety and well-being. But I saw no willingness (or ability?) to protect them from the animosity you express toward each other.

If your kids crash, as I fear they will, is it only their behaviors that will be addressed? For their sakes, might each of you be willing to seek a path to greater self-awareness and ask yourselves, "What's the payoff?"

Your daughters are learning from you how to live their lives.

Will you one day reap the whirlwind?

One Up, One Down

As the mediation session ended, Elizabeth put her arms around John, her husband, and hugged him. He stiffened but did not pull away.

The marriage of this handsome older couple was ending at her insistence. John, although restrained, made no effort to hide his anger. During several sessions he had ardently questioned the morality of having to share assets with a wife who chose to leave him, when he was without blame. And indeed she had made no accusation of wrongdoing on his part, no infidelity, no hint of physical abuse.

Both parties are highly educated professionals, she a retired college librarian, he a well-compensated corporate executive. Their children are long since grown. In my presence, they spoke to each other respectfully. Over the years they had worked with a counselor a number of times, but they agreed, unsuccessfully.

For a moment, Elizabeth's affectionate behavior confused me, but I recalled that when I earlier met with her alone, she had explained: "I simply have to get away, even though in some ways I still love him. He's been a good father and wonderful provider. But for thirty-two years, I've been subjected to his scorn. When no one else is there, I'm constantly belittled, even told that I'm stupid. Of course, he knows I'm not, but he needs to feel superior. No more. I'd rather be alone."

Had I not previously read about the work of the psychologist, John Gottman, now an emeritus professor of psychology at the University of Washington, I might have probed further. Gottman and his associates are renowned for their work on marital stability and divorce prediction. They record, and then analyze, three-minute video clips of recently married couples talking about a serious matter. They develop mathematical models. Then they forecast which of the couples will split up at some point in the next fifteen years. Follow up studies have proved their ability to make this prognosis with 90% accuracy.

When I first read about this, I was a bit skeptical. It almost seemed like a parlor trick, and Gottman is not without a few academic detractors. But I've come to believe it is not pseudo-science. When two hundred marital therapists and clinical psychology graduate students also viewed the three-minute clips, they could do no better than guess right 54% of the time, just above pure chance.

This data has been published in numerous peer-reviewed journals (citations available on *Wikipedia*). The scientific work is complex and beyond my ken, but for me the conclusions ring true.

Gottman and his team apply their equations to twenty separate emotional states observable in the brief videotaped conversations. He focuses on four predictors of marital failure: defensiveness, stonewalling, criticism, and contempt. The one he considers most important is contempt, which he says is qualitatively different from, and far more damaging than, the other three.

Contempt shows in words tinged with sarcasm, a glance that conveys disgust, personal insults, hostile humor or mockery, all delivered from a superior plane. It may be expressed in body language, the rolling of eyes or the very tone of voice. The expression of contempt is hierarchical, an assertion of one's power over another. The presence of contempt alone, according to Gottman, is the greatest predictor of marital collapse. (Contempt is hardly limited to failing marriages. No doubt it is equally destructive of relationships in the workplace.)

Interestingly, women tend to be more critical, while men are more likely to stonewall. But contempt is gender neutral: as many women as men manifest that power stance.

These are the very behaviors described by Elizabeth, who ultimately decided to end her marriage after so many years of what she now termed emotional abuse.

One up, one down. It drains away love.

Take It or Leave It

The eyes of the woman seated on my office couch brimmed with tears. At my request, her husband left the room for a few minutes. This was their third mediation session, and they'd been making steady progress, inch by inch, working out the terms for ending what had become a joyless marriage.

The decision to part had not been made lightly. For a time, they see-sawed back and forth and tried to reverse the downward slide with a skilled counselor. But now both seemed sure they were making the right decision. And once that direction was clear, a measure of calm had returned to their home.

So, I had reason to believe that their negotiation would continue to evolve in a positive way, although their property settlement was complicated by the need to assess the worth of the husband's business. They had chosen a valuation expert, but he had not yet submitted his report.

On this day, it became apparent at the outset that the husband's patience was spent. Just moments into the session, he abruptly presented a global settlement proposal and then forcefully said, "This is it---take it or leave it." His wife was surprised, remained silent, and looked to me for rescue.

When she and I were alone, I asked, "Do you know what brought on this change, the ultimatum?" She shrugged but understood my question. After breakfast that morning, she said, he had opened an invitation to their college reunion which had arrived the day before. Her husband had been a star athlete back then, the proverbial big man on campus. That was twenty years and thirty pounds ago.

While he had steadily climbed in the corporate world, nothing had matched those glory days. The reunion invitation appeared to enhance his "is this all there is" mood, which was, in part, the rationale for ending the marriage. Perhaps, she thought, this was what had sparked his change in demeanor.

Now that he had thrown down the gauntlet, we explored her choices. She could:

* Reject his proposal outright, which might mean terminating their negotiation;

* Argue that his position was unreasonable and try to convince him to await the valuation report;

* Let his demand pass without comment and help him find a way back to the table.

During my next brief chat alone with the husband, he disclosed little. Afterward we returned to the room where his wife awaited, where he sank heavily into the other end of the couch, his large frame somewhat more relaxed. She turned to face him and said, "I'm not sure but I think I may understand how you're feeling." The slightest nod of the head from him.

I shifted to talking about documents that still needed to be collected, and we made a plan for appraising the house. Neither he nor she nor I made any mention of his edict.

When we are verbally threatened with a "take it or leave it" demand, we are greatly tempted to respond in kind, sparking further escalation. The trigger for such a thrust may be a barbed remark or a perceived slight during the negotiation. But sometimes, as was the case here, an outside event can ignite an emotional state. Here he had laid down his ultimatum so early in our meeting that an outside source seemed likely.

Meeting an ultimatum by probing to understand the underlying cause, rather than confronting it head on, can preserve the path to eventually reaching agreement. Taking a short time-out, simply evading or side stepping the challenge, allows the belligerent one to calm down and save face. Forward motion can resume.

As they rose to leave, the wife addressed her husband, "Thanks for thinking things through to the point of designing a proposal. Talk it over next time?"

"Works for me," he said.

No smile, but I knew we were back on track.

Don't Count On It

She called to ask for the first available appointment. Could she and her husband meet with me without delay? They had been talking for some time about dissolving their marriage, and he was feeling guilty about an affair he'd had. He was proposing a generous settlement, and she wanted to "strike while the iron was hot."

For a moment I said nothing, thinking, *Don't count on it---guilt fades fast*. As if able to read my mind, she laughed, her voice tinged with a knowing sadness.

As a relationship is ending, the partner who perceives and portrays themselves as the injured party, may well get advice from family and friends to move forward quickly, to take full advantage of the other's guilty remorse. But experience has taught me that regret, even following an admission of fault, is a shaky foundation for lasting agreements.

I was able to schedule their first mediation session for the next week, and we began the process of defining their individual goals for the future. Both in their fifties and in good health, their children were grown and on their own. The story of the husband's culpability, spoken of early on, went unchallenged and hung in the air each time we met. Expectantly, I waited for his passive acceptance of blame to evolve into anger. But it did not. Although he chose not to share with me his motivation for leaving the marriage, he remained steadfast in his offer of substantial financial support for his wife for many years to come, in an amount significantly greater than he would likely be required to pay by the court. Was he simply biding his time while we worked out some of the asset valuation complexities of their case?

When promises earlier made are broken, a recent betrayal often becomes a focal point that is returned to time and again by the aggrieved partner. It's not uncommon in the early days to be simplistic and blaming. But most often, the breach that is initially seen as the cause of the marital rift is recast as the effect of numerous other expectations unmet, regrets and disappointments that have gone unattended or brought out in the open too late. Sometimes these mutual failings are a reality recognized only by one actor, although eventually both players often acknowledge personal attributes that contributed to the demise of their relationship.

I asked to meet with the husband alone, wanting to assure that he had sought the advice of experienced counsel, and that his decisions were well considered and that they would not crumble before pen was put to paper. I wondered aloud whether it was guilt or compassion that was motivating his largess.

"Does it matter?" he replied. "What's wrong with feeling guilty and doing what I can to put those thoughts to rest? I know the reasons for the failure of our marriage are not all of my doing. But this is less about looking back than about looking forward. I'm not atoning or even offering compensation. I want us both to get on well with life. With what I propose, she'll be secure, and I'll feel better about myself. So will our children. Leave it at that." I was chastened.

Consider all the jokes told about guilt-inducing mothers and the strict constraints imposed by early religious teaching. Don't they carry the message that mature adults are supposed to toss guilt aside? Here this man simply acknowledged his guilt for something he had done and was not proud of. Guilt's evil twin, shame, or even embarrassment, was not present. His admission spoke about his actions, not the essence of who he was. Would he still feel he made good decisions some years hence? Impossible to know, but in this case his values prevailed, respected by me and prized by his wife.

Guilt has gotten a bad name in our feel good age: We are to analyze its sources and exorcise it. Was I misguided in my cynical assumption that feelings of guilt, when met with blame, would ultimately fade and instead fuel anger, even retribution; and that the betrayal would shift from being a cause to being an effect? Instead, here guilt motivated compassion and recognition of a shared human frailty.

Anger: Serves You Well or Does You In?

I'm uneasy in the face of anger. In my professional world, I've learned how to manage that of others. But in my personal world, the anger I feel towards others, or if I am the target, can leave me a bit unhinged, at least for a while.

Therapists have helped many people to recognize and legitimize their anger. Some find that depression begins to lift and a new sense of self and autonomy is achieved, all to the good. But others, who I suspect give up that exploration too soon, wear their new-found acceptance of their angry feelings as a badge of courage, and it can do them in.

Consider this: A husband has been betrayed---his wife has met a new preferred partner. During the marriage he worked at home, fostered his wife's successful career, provided day care for the children, and kept the home fires burning brightly. Husband's anger is now given free rein, and fuels his days.

In the negotiation setting, divorcing parties frequently express anger, understandably so. This wife makes generous financial proposals, born, in part, of her remorse, but the husband angrily rejects them. To my cautionary words, he responds, "My therapist said I have every right to express my anger."

Meeting privately with him, I suggest that expressing anger in a therapeutic setting, or to a friend, may well serve a valid purpose, but it does not serve him well when negotiating. Whether one has the right to be angry is not the point. Reaching a favorable result is. So, I advise: taste the anger, but then become strategic.

My words fall on unreceptive ears. A quick turnaround appears impossible. I urge a return to therapy with a focus on his immediate situation. It may take months of litigation before he is able to recognize that his angry stance is self-defeating.

Recently, I received a letter from someone I did not know, criticizing a public affairs event I had a part in presenting earlier in the week. The letter was belligerent in tone and replete with misunderstanding. That night I lay wide awake at three a.m. mentally composing a heated response. I wanted to perfectly, artfully put him in his place. But hours later, in the light of day, I decided not to devote any more precious hours to venting my anger. Nothing of any importance would be gained. I was pleased and even a bit proud of myself to be able to let the matter fade away.

My personal epiphany occurred many years ago when a book by a self-help guru got me on the right track. He pointed out that holding on to anger at someone hands that person tremendous power. The target of your anger, in a sense, takes control of your life. That was the last thing I wanted.

CHAPTER FIVE

FRIENDSHIP

My Friend Dona

When spring finally arrives and forsythia gives way to daffodils and tulips, my thoughts return to another spring sixteen years ago, to vivid and poignant memories of events that occasioned insights that continue to serve me well. This is the story:

For several decades Dona and I were the closest of friends. We talked often during the week and took a long walk together almost every weekend, whatever the weather. There was little about our lives we did not share.

She had been coping with breast cancer for many years. But over the past year, she'd been on a downward slide. Now the narcotics used to dull her pain left her debilitated and sleepy much of the time

One early April day we were talking on the phone, and she asked me what I knew about hospice care. I told her of my experience gleaned from another friend and offered to help her research the issue further.

Then, without a pause or response, she changed the subject---to the birthday of her beloved seven-year-old granddaughter. She told funny stories about the gift she'd sent and the phone call she'd later received. When she grew weary of talking, we agreed to get together later in the day if she felt up to it.

The end of her life was approaching, and yet she had avoided discussing it. I loved Dona very much and could easily focus on what her loss would mean for me. But I said nothing of it to her, observing the unspoken taboo of acknowledging death's approach. The calm nature of our talk seemed both right and absurd. But that she had pointedly changed the subject to tell stories about her grandchild left me unsettled and confused. We had shared so openly with each other in the past, without barriers. My somber unspoken question was whether she really needed to talk more purposefully about dying and the plans she was considering.

Shortly afterward, I met a companion for a leisurely lunch. As we greeted each other, she noted that I looked troubled and asked how I was. "Confused," I responded.

She gave me her full attention, and I explained my quandary. Should I have colluded with Dona, I asked, in avoiding such a serious but painful and perhaps fearful discussion?

My wise companion said, "Why not just ask her whether she would like to talk more about her need to cope with the weeks ahead and how you might help?"

Of course. That was exactly what I needed to do.

Later that day, I visited Dona. As she lay on her couch, I sat close to her and I held on to her warm smooth ankle. We chatted amiably about mundane events and a medical test scheduled for the next morning. Our words were alternately light and serious. She got tired, but before I left, I leaned close and said: "I love you very much and want to help you through this in any way I can. So whenever you want to talk about making plans or anything else, will you call me?"

"I love you too," she said, "and I will call, but you call too, if I don't."

I assured her I would.

I left, no longer confused, knowing that the awkwardness of discussing death was gone, had been breached by my request and her invitation. We would no longer have to avoid what was uppermost on her mind and my own. We would be able to talk openly once again and be loving till the end.

Before Dona died, we did have a number of important and meaningful conversations. And afterward, her husband invited me to select anything I wished from her personal belongings. I left with a bottle of the scent she always wore, and I have worn it ever since.

Empathy Redefined

To pass along insights acquired from experience over the years is satisfying. But when applying such wisdom to events in my own life doesn't work, that is sobering.

In this case, the wisdom was: When another person's point of view or behavior is problematic or upsetting, quiet your tendency to be reactive. Stand in their shoes. Empathize. View the situation from their perspective. As a professional helping others, I can do this with reasonable dispassion. And many times I've said, "Once you empathize, you can sympathize with their point of view."

It's not always easy if I'm emotionally involved, but I thought I had even these situations figured out.

Some years ago my son and daughter-in-law divorced. I loved her dearly and still do. She lives far away, so we visit only occasionally, but we continue to correspond and speak on the phone. Often she shares her concerns with me and our words flow easily---unless she makes a negative comment about my son. But I can ignore these words if they are written, or remain quiet if they are spoken, and attend to the rest of her message. She is a quick study, so takes my silence into account and we move on, each of us accepting a well-established boundary that we cross only occasionally and then renew.

So empathy works, until it doesn't.

I have another dear friend, Jan, who lives some distance away, and over the years I've maintained a close connection with her and her husband, Jack. I consider them both to be intimate friends---he a former colleague of my husband. But one day I received an email from Jan complaining bitterly about her husband's behavior and attitude. Her tone clearly assumed I would be aligned with her---she was seeking both my sympathy and asking for my professional advice.

I was upset about being brought into their personal lives and resented being expected to take sides. My inclination was not to respond at all, but soon I knew that ignoring her message would be too unkind a rejection.

After mulling it over, I shared my quandary with a trusted colleague. I explained I could not simply accept Jan's perception of events and offer sympathy and advice without feeling disloyal to Jack. Nor was I willing to be drawn into the details of their intimate angst and make judgments about what went on.

As we talked, some new wisdom emerged: I was confusing empathy with the need to sympathize. Empathy requires only a willingness to hear and attempt to understand what someone has to say, not to embrace it. Sympathy, on the other hand, implies agreement and a readiness to become an actor in the play. With that distinction clearly in mind, I was able to frame a heartfelt response that was empathic and not rejecting.

A bit wiser now, I stepped back into my own shoes. Taking care of myself, I also asked Jan to see me only as a friend, which makes giving professional advice to either of them untenable. An important boundary was established.

A Gift from a Stranger

Friends no longer ask, "What did you get for Christmas?" Their children are grown, their shopping ventures minimized and simplified, a check, a book, or something sweet and consumable. I've become something of a humbug: Holiday presents are important only in memory when my family was young and the children's excitement contagious. I much prefer receiving an unexpected gift, unrelated to a ceremonial day, delivered as a simple token of affection.

Around the holidays a few years ago, I had an experience (which I relate below) that brought to mind a moving story of gifting by the famed Chilean poet Pablo Neruda. He wrote about an early childhood encounter when he lived in a house separated from that of a neighbor by a high fence. One day he noticed the small hand of a child pushing a toy through a hole in the fence, a tiny white sheep made of faded wool. Young Neruda did not know the child, who lived next door. Wanting to return the favor, he pushed his most favored pinecone through to his unknown benefactor.

He and the other child never met, but many years later Neruda wrote that this mysterious gift exchange stayed with him, gave his poetry its light. "To feel the affection that comes from those that we do not know [is] greater and more beautiful because it widens the boundaries of our being, and unites all living things," he wrote. "Just as I once left the pine cone by the fence, I have since left my words on the door of so many people who were unknown to me, people in prison, or hunted, or alone."

My remembered experience happened when I was leaving my local branch post office. Just as I reached my car, I witnessed a near collision in the busy parking lot. I drove off a bit shaken, and upon arriving at my next destination, I discovered that my wallet was missing. Thinking back, I realized that when I was distracted by the close call,

I'd placed my wallet on top of the car when opening the door and driven off. In haste, I returned to search the lot---to no avail.

Dismayed by the foolishness of my lapse and the loss, I began to mentally catalog all those facets of my life contained in that zipped leather packet. I dreaded the hours I would now have to spend alerting credit card companies, applying for a new license and membership identifications. The lost cash almost seemed inconsequential.

Home on my laptop, I began the process of notification, wresting some control from chaos. Then the phone rang. Caller ID revealed an unfamiliar number, which I was tempted to ignore, but I did not.

It was Lateefa Kituku. She'd found my wallet, which had fallen to the roadway several blocks from the post office. Knowing I would be upset, she assured me that everything inside was intact and safe. Instantly my gloom gave way to relief and gratitude. We agreed that I would pick it up the next morning at the office of the school where she is a kindergarten teacher. When I did so, I left a note of thanks for her and a gift for her classroom.

My elation went far beyond retrieving important bits of paper and plastic, my identity restored. Like Neruda's gift of the small toy sheep, this kindness from a stranger was more meaningful in many ways than a present received from a good friend, even one thoughtfully chosen and beautifully wrapped.

Neruda's words echoed. This gift, the kindness of a stranger, widened the boundary of my being. I felt united with a vast caring community.

Stepping into Another Life

In my youth, the only people we knew intimately were close friends and family members. We knew prominent persons only by the life they were willing to display in public, in newspaper coverage and occasionally the telling of an apocryphal story of some youthful adventure. It was by reading fiction that I could delve into another person's mind, vicariously experience their perceptions and emotions, and in this way step into a different life.

But in recent decades, society has become far more open, and memoirs are an ever more popular genre, among both celebrities and common folk. This is an unveiling I welcome. It adds richness to our knowledge both of others and ourselves, and it affords an understanding and empathy for the author, even when their experiences and beliefs are vastly different from our own.

A few years ago I read *My Beloved Country*, Supreme Court Justice Sonia Sotomayor's very personal story, and she became my new best friend. Obviously, a jest, but if she were to walk into my living room, I know our conversation would flow easily. We had a number of formative experiences in common: we both entered the law while it was still a mostly male profession; she spent years working as a prosecutor, which provided insights into the human condition similar to those I was gleaning as a public defender. But our differences are stark as well. We were born into and grew up in very different worlds, she in a Bronx housing project and I in middle-class Westchester County.

That Justice Sotomayor is now so well known affords me a greater connection to the high court than I ever had before. For when I entered law school in the 1960s, I barely knew that group of austere wise white men, except for their written opinions. Now I yearn to know more.

So I wonder, do the Justices come to know each other well? I know they frequently lunch together, for Justice Sotomayor told Oprah they break bread together at their midday meal. But do they share with one another an in-depth knowledge of their childhood and early family life, and how their current views evolved over time? If so, does friendship motivate them to converse respectfully with one another, to genuinely wish to understand each other's thinking, and to eschew labeling and discounting their opinions out of hand? I hope so, and think it might just be so.

More recently I read *My Grandfather's Son* by Justice Clarence Thomas, the only other currently sitting justice who has written a memoir. Even in the first half of this compelling book, I am getting to know him as well. Am I finding commonalities that allow me to relate to the most conservative justice on the bench? Few, until I reached his description of nervously awaiting his bar exam results. But his vivid telling of the harshness of his early family life, and the cruelties he experienced growing up in the segregated South affect me deeply. His evolution from a radical Democrat as a college student to conservative Republican is a fascinating story. The angry and bitter defiance that characterized his confirmation hearing has not softened over time, at least as of the writing of this book. He makes no effort to hide his dark side, in contrast to his telling of many strong friendships, built throughout his career, that endure.

Cynics suggest that memoirs are self-serving, a reinvention of the truth. To some extent this is so, for our memories of the past are surely selective and sometimes allow for confabulation. But the story being told in a memoir is what is important to the teller, is their remembered life, the essence of who they are, or aspire to be, today. One need not share another's political positions or philosophical bent to gain understanding from their unique narrative. Such insights defy stereotyping and demonizing, the traps that preclude meaningful communication or a clear grasp of the other's perspectives.

I'm wondering if Justice Thomas would be open to a friendly discussion of the points about which we differ. If he were to walk into my living room, the words might not flow so easily at the start, but I suspect that before long we too would have a meaningful, respectful conversation.

Please Wait

If I could be granted a wish, it would be that all my good friends, and members of my family, would die only after I do. It's a selfish and frivolous wish, which gives but momentary comfort, but such is the nature of wishes. We all have to leave, to follow other loved ones, but I want those I love to wait.

Pat, my college roommate, a friend for over fifty years, died recently. We did not see each other often, as she lived on the east coast. But when we did connect, it was as if no time had elapsed since the last time. Her husband and mine shared a love of fishing, so our visits were often planned around their boyish pleasures.

I loved getting those glimpses into her life, her long marriage to the man who caused many on our college campus to say they were sure it wouldn't last. We shared photos and stories of our children, the funny and the sad. We talked by the hour about how our lives were evolving, without the gloss so often added with someone less known or trusted. And then we cooked the fish.

Now that she is gone, what I remember most is the warmth of her smile and the throaty laugh that so often punctuated our conversations, even the serious ones. I ache for her lonely husband. For a time he will be in the arms of their children, and other friends and family will gather round, which consoles me. Then the empty house. Their dog searching for his other friend.

Pat and I first met in college, when we were randomly assigned to share sleeping and study quarters. There were no computerized selection programs in those days. So much talk, often in the dark of night, telling our stories, discovering similar values and temperaments that blended well.

College friendships are made so easily, as if breathing the same air brings kinship. Just at the time that we are leaving our family home, often on the heels of stressful adolescent separation wars, we fall in with new siblings of sorts, without any of the complexity of the sibling relationships we have left behind. No old baggage, starting afresh. We are able to create a new persona if we choose and share the excitement of paths yet to be taken.

Losing loved ones is as much a part of life as gaining them. I comfort myself by remembering the high of falling and being in love, of welcoming a new baby, the depth of other friendships which have grown over the years, and for a time it restores my equilibrium. But then I yearn to hear Pat's laugh and to hold her dear ones close, express my love, and share their sadness.

So, I wish that she had waited.

The Other Mother

Today my other mother died at the age of ninety-nine. Vicki was my father's kid sister, the aunt who was happy to take me in when I ran away from home. This is the story:

When I was twenty-two, she was in her early forties, ten years younger than my mother. Len and I had just graduated from college, and he was soon to embark on an advanced degree. For both strategic and financial reasons, he was spending the summer in the Nevada desert as field assistant to one of his soon-to-be Columbia professors. I was newly pregnant and this was not a good time for us to be apart. But I had a safe haven: parents who happily welcomed me home to await my husband's return.

This college graduate, wife, and soon-to-be mother became a child again---worse, an adolescent. My mother was a loving and generous woman, and in recent years we got along very well. But now, returned to living under her roof, I bristled as she suggested improvements: a haircut, perhaps a blouse of a more becoming color, a more cheerful presence.

Just weeks before, Len and I, pressed together in a street corner phone booth, had called with the exciting news of our expected baby, a first grandchild. Vivid in memory was the question she asked: "Was it planned?" Now I found I was unable to put aside the feelings it engendered.

So, I fled to the small white cottage of my aunt in Lakeville, Connecticut. Vicki, an editor at Doubleday, commuted weekly to New York City, returning home laden with manuscripts of aspiring authors. Recently divorced from her doctor husband, (he still beloved in our family), she was raising her young son on her own. Divorce was a rarity then, and though they did not say so, the family assumed she must have been at fault.

My mother and my aunt were loving competitors, first for my father's affection (and, of course, my mother won that round), and then for mine. Vicki was delighted to harbor her runaway niece, no doubt pleased to be the winner of this tug-of-war. Staying with her offered me the excitement of the publishing world and a glimpse into the life of an independent career woman, sophisticated and defiant. But most of all, she gave me unconditional acceptance.

Over the next thirty years, our relationship thinned as we both moved to distant states, and she remarried. We became close again after my mother's death in 1987, but my mother won the middle rounds.

How grand to be loved and welcomed without reservation by another mother, one who can offer the accumulated wisdom of the generation before, who can lavish tender care without the admonitions or questions that all mothers must labor to suppress once their children are grown.

I expect many of us can identify those non-parental adults---aunts, uncles, neighbors, or teachers---who took on the mantle of wise elder without the tensions inherent in the ties that bind parent and child.

Love and protection, offered while having no investment in another's perfection, can be a wonderful gift.

An Ethical Quandary

Sometimes when reading, I come upon a phrase so delightful, I jot it down to savor it at another time. It may perfectly describe a place or depict an emotion I have known. I momentarily yearn to make it my own, fully recognizing it as the creation of another writer's talent. Is my fantasy the seed of plagiarism? Even some of the mighty have fallen. These meanderings lead me to a story.

Last year a friend called to request a favor. Her daughter was applying to colleges and had drafted the required application essay. Would I be willing to read it over and make editing suggestions? Of course.

When I was quite young, I remember well, I asked my mother to review something I'd written. When she pointed to some misspelled words before offering me the hoped-for praise, I snatched the paper from her hands. The very fact that I retained this long-ago memory confirmed my friend's wisdom in seeking help from someone unrelated.

Days later I sat down with her daughter at their dining room table. We knew each other only slightly, so there was some discomfort, but little tension. I read her essay, and it brought tears to my eyes. She had written about attending the wedding of an older cousin some months before, then learning of his sudden death just weeks later. The joyous event, when her family came together from many parts of the country, was followed closely by the tragedy of an early death, and another coming together at the funeral. She wrote about life's uncertainties and her need to recognize and value what was precious to her rather than take it for granted.

The essay's structure was awkward in places, and certain words were overused, but it was, in essence, simple and beautiful. I suggested she reorder some sentences, remove certain phrases, and make some different word choices. In the end it seemed quite perfect, and we were both pleased. Months later my friend called to report that her daughter had been accepted at her preferred college, and I was gratified.

Then just weeks later Randy Cohen, whose admirable columns on ethics appeared weekly in *The New York Times*, responded to a question about whether a teacher should help a student seeking editing assistance with a college application essay. Unequivocally, Cohen said no.

For a moment, I wondered, *have I participated in a fraud?* I chose to think not, but I'm not sure.

Virtually every book published contains a credit that lauds the author's editor (and new best friend). Writers thereby appear to be more accomplished than they are and no doubt reap the financial benefits of another's skill. Lawyers routinely place their names on briefs written in large part by unidentified associates. How many judicial law clerks go unnamed? True, book editors are sometimes acknowledged, and the practice of writing legal briefs is well known. My role was not. But are there any college admissions officers who are unaware of the assistance given to applicants, indeed of all sorts of coaching they receive along the way?

I comfort myself with the knowledge that I in no way altered the substance of the essay. And if asked again for this kind of help, I think I would accede.

But an ethical question is presented, if not the consummate answer.

A Delicate Balance

Is it heresy to suggest that there are times when friends offer greater comfort than family? And that they are equally entitled to our attention and care?

On a recent evening, I watched an old film version of Edward Albee's Pulitzer Prize-winning drama, *A Delicate Balance*, which opened on Broadway in 1966 and which I happened to see in summer stock the following year. Albee assigned to his characters compelling statements about the conflicting demands and entitlements of friendship and family.

In their beautifully appointed home, Tobias and Agnes, an upper middle-class husband and wife, are in their sixties. Claire, Agnes's alcoholic sister, is a more or less permanent houseguest. As the drama begins, the often-married daughter, Julia, arrives, having just run away from her most recent marriage. Fueled by alcohol, the repartee is alternately loving and biting, the strain between family members intense.

Late in the evening the doorbell rings. Harry and Edna, another married couple have unexpectedly dropped in on their dearest old friends. Although Tobias and Agnes are surprised by their arrival, they welcome them warmly, until Harry and Edna calmly announce that they have come to spend the night, explaining only that while at their home they had become frightened. They retire to the guest room.

The next morning, to the relief of their bewildered hosts, Harry and Edna announce their plan to leave, but they make clear they are departing only to collect more of their belongings to move in indefinitely. Their fear remains undefined, referred to as "the terrors."

Thirty-six-year-old Julia reverts to an adolescent rant at being deprived of her old room (which is now the guest room). The family falls into disarray, and bitter arguments ensue. Tobias and Agnes are in turmoil. They are ambivalent about this imposition by their friends, while Julia and Claire, family members, have simply moved in, assuming their entitlement to do so.

The question posed: Does the forty-year close friendship with Harry and Edna require Tobias and Agnes to accept such an invasion of their already crowded home? It hardly seems so, but when Harry and Edna finally announce they are ready to depart, Tobias, weary after a sleepless night, urges them to stay. Their friendship, he fervently insists, entitles them to succor and protection in spite of the unexplained terror they have brought with them.

It is impossible to watch this story unfold without wondering what one's own response would be if dear friends arrived at the door, frightened, with suitcases in hand. How might we be treated if the terror was our own and we stood on our friend's threshold?

Many of my closest professional colleagues, who have also become dear friends, are far younger than I, some as young as my grown children. As with my older friends, my contemporaries, we have shared many milestones, both joy and grief. We know each other well and can count on an always-available listening ear, comfort when needed, and unconditional acceptance. These friendships, with their ease and pleasure, are free of judgment, and, for me, devoid of parental obligation or angst. With my children, I studiously monitor appropriate boundaries, but with my close friends that guardedness is not present. I can push or pull at will, even nag with impunity. My friends can accept or dismiss my admonitions, secure in the knowledge that our friendship will be unharmed. Only loving respect is called for, and that is well established. Advice is sought, or given without having been sought. We have no ancient history to cope with, no sibling rivalry, no family secrets.

As a young woman, I ran off to stay with a dear aunt when parental concern and criticism, spoken or only implied, became onerous. Many people I know have come to value these pseudo-parental or pseudo-child friends or relatives who offer the rewards of closeness with someone of an older or younger generation without the familial over-lay of either expectation or obligation.

Home is sometimes defined as family who have to take you in when you have nowhere else to go. Maybe so. But should the terrors descend and we seek comfort, perhaps we might be more at ease with dear friends.

Just Being There

Sometimes just being a silent presence, or even promising to be present, can make a difference.

A married couple were parting ways. Making the decision took many months, but at the end both acknowledged that their efforts to change and please the other failed, so they sought me out to mediate the end of their marriage. In preliminary phone conversations, each told me that the blaming was over, but important financial decisions had yet to be made. They had tried to reach common ground, had sat together at the kitchen table and talked over coffee. But as he probed, she fell silent. Their efforts had evoked old miseries and tensions. So, they decided to come and sit with me.

Once they were in my office, a safe place, conversations that they had previously withheld flooded out. I directed the verbal traffic, turning first to one, raising an eyebrow at the other, but I remained silent and took notes. I added barely a word here or there, nothing of substance. My wisdom was all but superfluous. Quite on their own they talked through their issues and reached new understandings. The road forward cleared. Their earlier promise of civility was kept.

My very presence, listening to the Ping Pong of their earnest conversation, offering but a hand gesture now and then, was the gentle restraint that kept the talk from being derailed by emotion and allowed them to listen and really hear what the other needed to say.

··········

I sat by the bed of a dying friend who was in and out of consciousness, by turn calm and agitated. When she opened her eyes and met my gaze, I asked her if there was anything I could do for her. She told me she'd written but not yet delivered a check for her son's birthday. Could I see that he received it? Of course. Did I imagine that she then eased as we just continued to hold hands, until her husband returned? I was comforted just being there, and think she was as well.

· · · · · · · · · ·

Garrison Keillor told a story about the years he attended Lake Wobegon High School. He had a "storm home." Some residents of the town volunteered to provide emergency shelter during the cold winter months. Each youngster was assigned a specific house to go to in the event a blizzard made it impossible to get to their own home in the countryside. Many times he walked past the house selected for him, he said, picturing the people who lived there. He did not know them but hoped one day he'd be welcomed as part of their family for a day or two. It never happened. But Keillor talked warmly of that safe place, imagining an offer of hot chocolate, a crackling fire in the hearth as the wind howled outside, and he cozy and secure with them. He said his troubles were more bearable just knowing he had a storm home to go to.

· · · · · · · · · ·

So if a dear friend offers to be present should a crisis arise, or at a lonely time, they may never have to be called upon, but how comforting to be told: *Be sure to call if you need me.* The promise to be present, to open their door---we all need the assurance of a hand to hold, someone to just be there, a storm home. What a wonderful gift to offer another.

Men Friends

Living alone now after a near lifetime of intimacy with a partner, friendships are my mainstay, and my gratitude for close connections with others soars. Missing Len brings to mind his good fortune to have male friends, although there were times I secretly denigrated his friendships with men as somehow less significant than mine with women.

My close friends have always been confidantes. His were companions with whom he joyously went fishing or flying or explored the wilderness. Upon his return, if I quizzed him about conversations they'd had or intimacies shared, his answers were brief, relating stories told of other adventures, but little I deemed of substance. They'd said nothing of their marriages, troubled relationships with grown children, or problems at work--- the very essence of my exchanges with women friends, offering support, and seeking insights.

Men just talk less to each other. Everyone accepts this reality. Most don't share feelings with other men, beyond elation or frustration at a good or bad catch. Women smile knowingly, sometimes smugly, and express regret about valued experiences men are missing.

Reasons abound, genetic, hormonal, cultural---likely all three. Most people my age, even those much younger, were raised and nurtured by women, so that is the feminine model for intimacy. Men are more competitive, and from boyhood they are encouraged to be tough and strong. If a man has something to gain in a competitive environment, power or money, he will not reveal weaknesses. He will have no basis for trust unless others show him theirs.

I know I overgeneralize, and some older and many younger men may not fit this paradigm today. At least I hope they do not (and I plan to query my sons about this when they visit). I can't help but wonder if most men are still missing out on the richness that self-disclosure affords, instead of relying on their attachments to women for this reward? It would seem so.

Then why, despite male emotional reserve, was Len so fortunate? For four years, he refused to allow his Parkinson's to impact his life significantly, but in his final year he had to succumb to the use of a walker and eventually a wheel chair. This meant he had to give up his treasured pilot's license. Vulnerability that was previously hidden could no longer be denied. His passion for flying and fishing was defeated, beyond reach.

But two of his friends did not let this happen. Alan Wolfson, the man who bought his small plane, called often and suggested Len meet him at the airport and come along on a flight. It was no mean task to hoist his nonresponsive legs into the passenger seat, where dual controls allowed him to actually copilot on their journey.

And Len's longtime devoted fishing friend, Jim Hoffmeister, remained a constant presence in his life, coming often to pick him up, wheeling him to his van, and driving off for an adventure. Usually they returned by nightfall, but just months before Len died, Jim became his caretaker as well as his companion on a trip north to a frozen lake where they fished through the ice for days on end.

Using female standards to appraise male friendships may miss the mark. Do they become known to each other by their shared experiences and so build trust and caring? Len's friends may have known little of sharing intimacies with words, but of love they knew everything.

A Troubled Friend

One of the great joys of getting older is friendships that span decades, in which you are so well known that you don't need to defend yourself when feeling vulnerable or when weaknesses are exposed---and being able to offer the same unqualified acceptance to another.

Paul and I talk often since the death of his wife four years ago---she had been a good friend of mine as well. Last year Paul, in his early seventies, retired and in robust health, became intimate with another woman and reveled in his new found love. She, eight years younger and still engaged in her work, also expressed delight about their coming together.

But now the bloom was fading.

We met to share a meal, and his description of their recent conversations was disturbing. Angry outbursts on her part were now frequent. She did not return his phone calls for days, and should he call a second time, she berated him for being too intrusive. Yet he persisted. He seemed captivated and unwilling to give up this connection, but the puzzling unpredictability of her behavior was causing him anguish and many sleep-disturbed nights. He'd been losing weight and wasn't looking well.

I offered only a listening ear, having long ago learned not to take on the role of armchair therapist with troubled friends. But I did urge him to consult a skilled professional. Initially he resisted the idea, but eventually he took that advice and let me know he found the experience both reassuring and enlightening.

But the abusive (my unspoken view) relationship continued.

When we met again, he talked of having gained insight into her behavior: He now viewed her actions as less a function of who he was, and more as a serious deficit of her own. He and his counselor were also exploring why he accepted such harsh treatment so willingly. The question he asked me was, "How does becoming more self-aware translate into being better able to cope?"

For he was still often miserable and mired in the past, reviewing and dissecting their conversations and the pain of rebuke.

Now I did have something I wanted to offer, so putting all caution aside, I told him that some years ago I read about cognitive behavior therapy (CBT). Over time I learned how to practice it for myself at times of anxiety or mild depression. About this I unashamedly proselytize, so I said:

"You claim your emotions have been pretty much out of control. Now that you are more self-aware, you can examine your reactions to disturbing events and identify the thoughts that arise and determine your mood. The trick is to question whether those thoughts are flawed in some significant way. For example, are you drawing conclusions by assuming you know what is in the minds of others? Are you predicting the likelihood of future events without sufficient evidence? Does a single event push you into all-or-nothing thinking? These are distorted ways of thinking, not rational thoughts that can lead to a sound plan for the future. You may now be ready to do this analysis."

It all sounded good to me, even if a bit academic. But from Paul I just received a quizzical look and a cautious *maybe.*

Weeks passed, then Paul and I met for an early breakfast. He told me the relationship was dwindling, though it had not yet ended. But he had a new tone in his voice, his bearing was more erect, and I noted that the future tense crept back into his conversation.

He made no mention of CBT as part of his repertoire. I will give up on that pitch to him, as I have with others who smile and nod at my ardor and soon change the subject. It is our friendship, not my unsolicited advice, that serves us well.

CHAPTER SIX

MARRIAGE AND PARTNERSHIP

Soul Mates: Myth Or Reality?

One evening I shared dinner at my home with a friend I've become close to in the years since the death of my husband. She never knew Len, but I often spoke to her about him, about us.

On this evening, I showed her a collage of photos taken at different stages of our marriage: in our college years, with small ones on our laps, on family vacations, and after we were once again on our own, the children grown. Like most family photos on display, they show us all smiling, our children attractive, our arms entwined, all of us happy together.

She commented, "You two were soul mates, weren't you?"

I was surprised by this. I don't remember my response, probably just a somewhat hesitant nod. We had also been talking about her marriage, which seemed fine overall, but on this night her words were tinged with disappointment.

Weeks went by before we met again. In the interim, I thought often about her use of the term *soul mates* and was troubled. It was not a phrase I would have used.

For more than fifty years, Len and I loved each other well, most of the time. But we were not soul mates, as I understand the meaning of this New Age term, totally compatible perfect halves of a whole, fated to be together, intimates speaking the same language.

That was not our reality.

In his absence, as I miss him so, it is the better times that most often come to my mind and that I talk about. But I didn't want my friend to look to us as an ideal for comparison, against which she might find cause to be discouraged about her own marriage when they were cycling through a trying time.

I needed to tell her that the ideal is a fiction.

Michelle Obama did this well. Untold articles have been written about the Obama marriage. Pictures of them holding hands and smiling have been beamed to every corner of the globe. How my admiration for her grew on reading a 2010 *New York Times Magazine* article in which she was candid about unhappy interludes.

The image of a flawless relationship is "the last thing that we want to project," she said. "It's unfair to the institution of marriage, and it's unfair for young people who are trying to build something, to project this perfection that doesn't exist."

As the years went by, Len and I came to accept that we did not share many of each other's interests. We set aside the romantic dream that somehow we could be all things to each other. Over time we became more autonomous as we alternately fostered each other's careers and longings. Our mutual attraction and respect, and our growing family, were the glue that carried us through the difficult days.

Most often when we were out of sync, we each muddled through on our own, all the while struggling with our very different communication styles (I owe a special debt of gratitude to Professor Deborah Tannen for writing *You Just Don't Understand*.) And occasionally, we enlisted a therapist to offer a different lens, a new perspective.

Invariably, confronting unhappiness brought us closer.

Now, looking back, it's tempting for me to generalize from my personal experience when friends comment on or ask about our long successful marriage. But respecting the unique personalities and circumstances of others, I desist. It suffices to say we were lucky to have met, to have shared a determination to problem solve, and to have had a love that carried us through the scary times.

But we were never soul mates.

Fear That Does Not Fade

Having decided to write about violence and intimidation between intimate partners, my heartbeat quickens and I'm tempted to stop before I've begun. I've never been subjected to physical abuse or the rage of another who sought to control my actions, so I don't fully understand why I so readily insert myself into the stories I hear. Do others do the same, then try to escape, to evade the feelings that arise?

When mediating with those whose marriage is ending, I strive to offer a safe setting, one in which both parties feel empowered and able to speak freely. To that end, on the day of our first meeting, I always talk briefly with each person alone, and one veiled question I ask is "How did you resolve disputes during your marriage?"

Not often, but sometimes one partner will disclose a grievous assault, or behavior that was so controlling that even when no hand was raised to do physical harm, furious words that repeatedly devalued and demeaned had much the same impact, even when softly spoken.

I always wonder, *Why didn't you leave?* I never pose this thoughtless question out loud, but many others have, for without prompting, the victim will often offer a well-practiced justification:

I knew I could handle it.

The children needed their father.

I didn't want anyone to know, the shame of it.

She demeans my every move, tells me I'm a fool and have no backbone, but it's just words.

If arrested he would have lost his job.

He was going through a bad time and promised it would never happen again.

Oddly enough, the speaker of these unspeakable rationalizations remains calm, while I strive to maintain my composure. I'm relieved to accept these reassurances and end this discussion. And move on.

In fact, over the years, I've successfully concluded a number of mediated cases in which one partner reported experiencing threats and rough treatment, or angry controlling behavior that stripped them of dignity and self-esteem. They developed coping behaviors that allowed the marriage to survive for many years and even an appearance of normalcy. I took at face value the notion that one could erase, forgive and set aside the past, or even forget it.

Now, I know better. And I ask myself: *How many of those prior agreements were motivated and settled under the specter of fear?*

Today, I'm better schooled and wiser. Experiencing purposefully inflicted pain and living in dread of an intimate partner have a lasting impact. I no longer listen passively to the rote explanations, nod, and move on. I press for details, and when I do, the anxiety, theirs and mine, arises anew. This is what I hear:

We were on a Sunday drive on a winding road, and I asked him to slow down. His right arm swept across the space between us, breaking my nose.

We were in the cellar examining the furnace, which had gone cold. I checked the sticker, and when I noted aloud that the inspection was overdue, he broke my arm.

Even in front of others, she repeatedly insults me and challenges my manhood.

He never touched me, but after crushing my cell phone underfoot, he stood in the doorway and wouldn't let me leave the room.

Now I probe: "Are you still afraid? Do your friends and family know? Are you seeing a counselor?"

In almost every instance, residual fright is admitted, and tears flow. Negotiating with their partner, even in my presence, the power imbalance takes hold. So, except in rare cases where the passage of time and significant therapy have provided new strengths, I know that my skill as a mediator cannot overcome the impact of enduring intimidation. Mediation must end and a different path be taken.

Those who grow up in homes where there is raging and coercion, I'm told, often seek to connect with partners who are controlling and sometimes physically violent. The terrible irony for some is that we seek an adult life consistent with our early experience. Those who were well loved presume they will be protected and treated with respect. Those who were frightened accept living with fear. But when someone in a relationship that is charged with intimidation finally has the courage to leave, they should have a lawyer-advocate negotiating at their side to assure safe passage to a well-reasoned settlement, forged in a secure setting, and protected from the fear that does not fade.

When Life Just Happens

Too often it is only after years of sidestepping talk of their discontent, that partners openly and seriously explore their thwarted desires. Much that might be timely addressed goes unsaid until it is too late.

Here is the story a divorcing couple recently told. Seventeen years earlier, the wife had become pregnant, they married, and she gave up her plan to attend college. He achieved career success, making it unnecessary for her to take a job for pay.

As the family grew, they moved to an upscale suburb where the children attended private schools. Although she still yearned to return to serious study, she said little of it as obligations at home and in the community filled her days.

After a time, he felt trapped in a career he would happily have left, but for the need to support their expensive lifestyle. The immensity and seeming impossibility of fulfilling their dreams overwhelmed them both, although occasionally their discontent was the subject of aimless late-night talks. With all passion spent, they had drifted apart. They didn't blame each other for the disappointments they now openly discussed, both suggesting: *It just happened.*

Some years ago, a friend introduced me to a small volume, *How to Get Control of Your Time and Life* by Alan Lakein. It's one of many books I never finished, but the early pages contained a suggestion I took to heart. Following the author's instructions, each year, usually in January, I sit before a blank piece of paper and without allowing any time for rumination, spend just two minutes writing the answer to each of the following questions:

1) What do I want to accomplish over the next five years?

2) What do I want to accomplish over the next year?

3) How would I spend the next six months if I knew I had only six months to live?

I've kept my annual lists and from time to time, I look back. Sometimes, with pleasure, I note goals that I have met. Other times I recognize that year after year I repeat the same objective without much forward movement. My answers to the third question are quite specific but the least likely to have been implemented. Denial?

I never share my lists with anyone. But many conversations with friends and colleagues are spawned with my aspirations in mind, and projects designed. Trying to enlist my husband to join me in this specific question and answer process failed. It wasn't his style. But over the years, my formalizing of goals, long and short term, often led us to talk about our dreams and miseries. We gave each other permission and support to initiate change, and many important changes were made.

But what happened to the two people seated on my office couch who spoke of their regrets, as they made plans for lives apart? At an earlier time, they felt great attraction for each other, and probably shared many values, yet they failed to seriously talk about or support each other's longings. Their imaginings about a different way of life were defeated before they were realistically explored.

What if they had asked each other how steps in new directions might have been taken, over the next six months or the next year?

Perhaps every couple, or at least one partner, should go through an annual assessment of what they wish they could do or be, to see if articulating what one hopes to achieve, might lead to important disclosures by both, and support for those ends.

When Talking Is Difficult

When colder weather approaches, I am reminded of a recent winter when my car broke down. It proved to be a failure not only of the mechanism but of my spirit, at least temporarily. For I felt ill equipped to cope with the decisions that had to be made.

Auto repair had always been Len's domain, not mine.

I managed well enough with the help of friends, and those who towed and repaired showed kind tolerance for my ineptitude. But what a stark reminder of the division of responsibility in our marriage. Although we often consulted with each other, decisions about the purchase or repair of anything with moving parts were left to him, interior design left to me. Insurance was his. Kid's clothing and wellness care were mine. With career decisions, he made his and I made mine. But major concerns, like a possible move to another city, a home purchase, or a child's blue mood, were always talked through to resolution. If memory serves me well, our shared values usually made these conversations easy, but not always.

Len piloted his own small plane. When he began to take our young grandchildren aloft, I developed a twitching eyelid and my sleep was seriously disturbed. We tried to talk about it. He was angry and hurt that I would question his judgment, and thought my fears irrational. I thought not, but even if they were, I needed to find a healthy way to cope. We knew this was an issue we had to confront and resolve, but my anxiety and his defensiveness made it a difficult conversation that went nowhere.

Eventually, we sought professional help, and along the way learned a lot about each other and ourselves. The outcome we reached was a compromise which I accepted gratefully, and he somewhat grudgingly: He would always take another pilot along when the grandchildren were passengers.

These meandering recollections bring to mind how often, in my practice, both partners who are approaching divorce maintain that whenever conflict loomed, too discouraged or unable to talk it through, they were the one who abdicated the decider role and simply gave in to the other. The moments they most clearly remember are those when a dream was compromised, eroding a sense of self, thwarting authenticity.

On the first day I meet with a mediating pair, I speak with each of them privately and ask how they resolved disputes during their marriage. How did they negotiate? Here is the interesting twist. Often each spouse reports that they were the one who most often capitulated and accommodated to the wishes or demands of the other. Both assert: "I just went along to get along." As impossible as this might seem, I think both parties are sincere in voicing this belief.

My friends whose relationships are working well readily acknowledge that they and their partner divide up decision making, leaving the prominent role in certain areas to one or the other. For them, talk is usually easy. But in a relationship that is ending, self-disclosing feels risky, talking is difficult, and their yearning to better understand each other is trumped by their anxiety or disappointment.

Without some intervention, preferably with an experienced counselor, dissatisfaction just grows and grows. And, of course, the earlier help is sought, the better.

To Go or To Stay?

My friend Anne rummages in her purse, then pauses, smiles, and remembers that she no longer smokes. It's a tense moment and she wishes she still did. After a deep sigh, she says, "Tim tells me that he just needs some space and is suggesting we try living apart for a while. What do you think?"

For some months now, I've been aware that this marriage was troubled, although Anne was sure they both still valued their bond. Her husband had rejected counseling, determined to protect their privacy and insisting, not without some bitterness, that he didn't need to "get fixed". I cautioned her, "If respectful conversations are still possible, give it more time. Separations usually become permanent."

I realized as I spoke, that although invited to give advice, I had no sound knowledge base for my statement, no actual data to support my conclusion, so I added that caveat.

All of the evidence from my professional life was anecdotal. Those who separated and then reconciled did not end up discussing divorce on my office couch, so my evidence was not only imperfect but also skewed. Yet many of my divorce mediation clients reported having separated for a trial period, sometimes for as long as a year, only to later decide to end the marriage.

For many, I surmise, proposing a temporary parting is often a way of letting their partner down easy, suggesting only the need for space but knowing they have made the decision to end the marriage. For others, I believe that the motive was more sincere, that they proposed separation as a testing time. But what was being tested---whether solitude was preferable?

When I quizzed a friend who had been a Magistrate in the Domestic Relations Court, she gave me another perspective on separations. In many of the dramas that had played out informally in her courtroom, she said, one spouse had previously suggested, or asked, or even demanded, that the other leave, only to later acknowledge that their real intent in suggesting a separation had been to test the commitment of their partner. Meanwhile the departed spouse became happier living on their own and declined to return. A risky request had probably been made impulsively, in a moment of hurt or anger.

I shared my personal experience with my friend, for I well remember those times during my own marriage when we were both unhappy, if not always at the same moments. It was toughing out those difficult days, struggling to understand and to be understood, that repeatedly brought us to a new and better place. We took long walks, sometimes together, sometimes alone. There were tears but also love, because we had opportunities to reconnect with spontaneity. We could reach out and touch, smile, or fix a favorite meal, do something to bridge the gap, then begin again to talk. But others within my family have taken a different path---they lived apart for a time, then came back together.

On balance, I've come to believe, even without reliable evidence, that when unhappy partners remain committed and respectful, they work out most problems best in close proximity, ideally with professional help.

Although I know there are exceptions that prove, or probe, this rule, is it not also true that nature abhors a vacuum? How often does the intimacy vacuum created by a separation get filled with new directions, new confidants, and new connections?

When There Is No Trust

Paula sat as if braced for a blow, unsmiling and on her guard. At the other end of my long office couch, Tom was her reverse image, comfortably relaxed.

It was not until I met with Paula alone that she gave voice to her anxiety. "He wants this divorce," she said in despair, "and I don't trust him anymore."

Her husband, a businessman, had taken the first step and walked away from what she acknowledged was not a happy marriage. The roles they took throughout their twenty-five-year union were well-defined, he the breadwinner and she in charge at home. They rarely crossed over into the other's world. Tom knew so much more than she did about finance---about their finances. How could she possibly negotiate with him, when she felt she couldn't rely on his having concern for her well being anymore?

Trust had been their bedrock, even as their intimacy faded. No longer.

"I do all the bill paying," Paula went on, "so Tom says I have a good grasp of money matters. Not so. He assures me I'll be fine, but I no longer have confidence in what he tells me."

"Why should you?" I asked.

She looked up, surprised.

"When an intimate relationship ends," I continued, "trust flies out the window, and anxiety sweeps in. Betrayal, broken promises or shifting moral standards, and a partner so well known becomes a stranger. The pain of loss and fear of the unknown dominates the emotional landscape. Then all that's needed is a spark, a canceled credit card, a barbed letter from an attorney, or finding out that a separate bank account has been opened. Any residual trust vanishes. Being assured that everything will be all right offers little solace."

Paula listened intently. "Do I need to hire a more aggressive lawyer?" she asked.

"That's one option," I said, "although I'd recommend you take the time and collect the information you need to become stronger and wiser yourself. An attorney who's committed to settlement might help you figure that out."

Her eyebrows rose, but she was smiling.

To those who've survived this early stage of divorce without declaring war, and have found their way into a mediation setting, or who've hired lawyers who can advocate for them while seeking consensus, and who recognize the need to address the interests of both parties, this is what I say: "Let's just assume that your spouse is untrustworthy. This is your current perspective. You may be wrong, but you may be right. So why not simply accept the absence of trust and design a settlement that doesn't depend on faith? Assert your power to say a respectful no to anything that is suggested, until you are ready to say yes. Ask for documentation and test proposed solutions assisted by carefully selected experts, lawyers, and financial planners. Decide to make no decisions until they are fully informed decisions. Let doubt serve you. You have no call to be accusatory or disrespectful. Just smart."

In marriage we expect trust. We assume that we'll always be told the truth and that our well-being will be given priority. That perfection may not always exist, but it's a reasonable expectation.

When an intimate relationship ends, aggression is not the answer, but trust need not be assumed---unless and until it is regained.

The Greatest Gift

The best gift I ever received was not my husband's to give, but was gratefully accepted; permission to change my life.

For six weeks in the summer of 1964, Len was exploring Scandinavia with a group of academic geologists, our longest separation in fifteen years of marriage. As his return drew near, the three kids and I drove about the country visiting friends and family, ending our journey at LaGuardia Airport, peering through a wall of glass, eager to spot him in the long line of weary travelers navigating customs.

Reunited, we headed for an airport hotel. All five of us tumbled onto the big bed, filling the air with our stories. The kids eventually settled down on rollaway cots. Len and I held each other close, wordless, as they drifted off to sleep.

The next morning we started home, the windows of our '57 Chevy station wagon open to the warm wind of late summer. Taking a road trip with a geologist presents the challenge of drawing his interest away from the rock and land formations he finds ever fascinating. Perhaps Len's divided attention gave me the courage to remark, my tone casual and tentative: "I'm thinking about going to law school."

Leading up to this moment, there is a story to be told: I was thirty-five years old. Julia, our youngest, would soon enter kindergarten. Concentrating fully on raising children gave me a satisfying sense of purpose, but as they got older, motherhood as a career was no longer enough. Len and I had talked about what I would do next. I could renew my teaching certification, but I'd been living in a child-centered world for twelve years and yearned for something else. But what?

One evening during our travels while Len was away, I had dinner with a friend whose wife was in the same quandary. He surprised me by asking if I'd ever considered law school. I hadn't, but the idea was born, and as I mulled it over during the days that followed, it took shape. I spoke of it to no one. Len's approval was the missing piece.

I often think back to that important moment on the Pennsylvania Turnpike in 1964, remembering who I was then, and I wonder how my life might have played out differently had Len not responded, "Law school? What a great idea. Perfect for you."

I was not without qualms when I presented him with my plan. For so many years law was an all-male profession, and it was assumed without question that there was some sound reason for it. Would challenging that premise undermine my desirability as a woman, as Len's wife? In 1949, the year we married, even college-educated women married young and welcomed home and hearth as their destiny. To put things in perspective, we married fourteen years before Betty Friedan wrote *The Feminine Mystique* and sparked the second wave of the women's movement.

Today, when law school enrollment of women equals that of men, my story may be but a faded relic of the past. Do women still pay attention any longer to maintaining the delicate balance of men's expectations and their own fulfillment? Do women still seek the approval of a loved partner before making a major identity shift? Do men? Or is it the essence of equality to no longer do so?

Surely fewer men than women interrupt or modify their careers when children arrive. Would they, if that was the gift that was sought? And when they do, or elect not to, how do those careers and marriages fare? We know that both men and women relinquish some competitive edge professionally when they take on the role of nurturer, either fully or shared.

How many professionals in positions of power---managing partners of law firms, corporate leaders---whose children are well launched, consider the dilemma of younger colleagues, female or male, facing these choices and ask themselves what accommodations they might make in the interest of better outcomes for all concerned? Is this the new arena for the gender wars?

But who is the new parent's adversary, their spouse or their employer? Do those making hiring decisions, or perhaps more importantly seeking to retain valued staff, make their judgments with traditional gender roles in mind? If so, I suspect their choices may no longer be wise ones, even for the bottom line.

Why Marry?

For the first time in more than one hundred years, the number of young adults (age twenty-five to thirty-four) who have never married has surpassed those who are. Of course, many of the unmarrieds are living with a partner without ceremony or license. The past taboo against that, at least for them, is ancient history.

And the divorce rate is declining. Is this good news or simply a reflection of the reality that fewer people are getting married?

And why should they?

Friends of mine have posed this question: Not just young people, but some in their middle years and even beyond and who are in committed relationships. I tell them about the legal protections afforded those who marry, and they listen, but they really want to talk about the more intangible benefits, or deficits, of marriage. They are wondering whether it will strengthen their treasured relationship or put it at risk? Will their bond become a bind?

Since I married over sixty years ago, this question never surfaced for me. But if urged to express an opinion, I opt for marriage, knowing well that it is my personal experience that leads me there. But I do wonder if it's simply an outdated romantic concept on my part.

A vivid memory: Just a year or so after we married, I walked alone across campus in a wintry drizzle. Len had been remote for a few days and I, only twenty-one years old, assumed it was because he was unhappy with me. I was flooded with dread, not for the loss of our love, but rather wondering how I could possibly tell my parents if our marriage should fail. By evening, all was well again.

In the years when our children were young, even if Len and I were out of sync and one of us sometimes dejected, the thought of divorce was kept completely at bay.

But the decades when our kids were in their teens, the 1960s and 1970s, the shifts in social conventions were profound, seismic. Casual sexual intimacy was becoming the norm, monogamy in marriage was called into question, and the divorce rate soaring. At some moments I mused that our marriage might feel like a cage, but was that very cage not also the structure that roused us to do the work to weather changing times?

Then after our last chick left the nest, we had twenty-seven years together. Would we have found a way to continue to support our ever-evolving relationship, if we had not been married? How can I really know? Happily, the love, joyous times and determination were always greater than the angst, and we kept our balance.

I've asked friends in their fifties and sixties, some married, others not, why they chose the path they did.

Said one: "We gave it serious thought and at first planned to marry, but in the end we knew that even though our love and trust was complete, trying to jointly manage some aspects of our lives as a married couple could cause serious conflict. Now, sixteen years later, the vows we exchanged over the kitchen table are just as enduring as if they were recorded at the courthouse."

Said another: "We knew we wanted to openly declare our love and commitment to each other and celebrate that with our friends. Marriage was the right answer for us, and we never considered another course."

Said another: "Wonderfully happy in my relationship, I agonized over the decision to marry, knowing I would first have to shake off the wrongheaded model of marriage handed down to me by my father. I finally did."

My generation had no such choice. If we wanted to be together, it was either marriage or scandal. Now the boomers are well into their middle years. Having come of age during the sexual revolution, encouraged by many a pied piper to openly defy parental values, even the vast majority who reentered the mainstream likely feel free to shape their love relationships to their own design.

I suspect for many women, perhaps most, the evolutionary pull for the protected nest and gravity's pull of aging gives the formality of marriage a certain import.

And I suspect for many men, perhaps most, settling down and resisting the evolutionary pull to impregnate far and wide, actually offers greater freedom to relax and focus on a satisfying union.

Those who advocate for a return to family values as strictly defined in years past may rail at the erosion of the marriage rules, but the genie of free choice is smiling and will not likely slide back into the bottle.

Beset By Uncertainty

He is casually dressed, smiling, and appears relaxed, but she is grim. Over a year ago he lost his job, a well-paid executive position. She is now working three part time jobs but earning little. His severance pay is spent, his unemployment compensation will soon end, and their savings are dwindling. Retirement funds are the next source to tap.

They've long since come to terms with ending their marriage: Both are emotionally ready to move on without rancor about the past. But her frustration with his apparent easy acceptance of being unemployed is clear. She says he is not worrying enough, no longer making a serious effort to find work, is too comfortable receiving benefits, playing golf, and drinking too much.

He listens and does not react, arms spread wide across the back of the couch. His enduring smile seems to me a nervous cover, and I wonder if he is immobilized by repeated rejection and his anxiety hidden but high. Her anger, fear really, flows from their unknown financial future, for college costs loom for both of their children, and their ongoing expenses erode their hard-won security. They are mired in uncertainty.

I've recently read that worry about the unknown is what does us in. Although it's counter-intuitive, bad news is easier to take than the possibility of bad news. Researchers have shown this to be true.

In a study conducted at Maastricht University in the Netherlands, the members of two sample groups were informed they would receive twenty electrical shocks. One group was told that each shock would be intense. The other group was told that three of the shocks would be intense, seventeen mild. Those in the second group sweated more profusely, and had a more rapid heartbeat, than those in the first.

A University of Michigan team studied patients whose colostomies were permanent and compared them to a group that had been advised there was a chance their colostomy could someday be reversed. The first group tested as being happier than the second who lived with hope for reversal.

Another study found that those who opt for genetic testing and get a result indicating they are at risk fare better than those who know their family history places them at risk but decide not to find out where they stand.

It seems that once we get bad news, we adapt and work at making the best of it. But waiting for bad news that might come keeps us in a worrisome state that undermines our well-being.

My personal solution when unsettled by disturbing news is to give myself over to fretful rumination for about twenty-four hours. I imagine the worst possible outcome and contemplate what survival will look like and what consequences I might have to face. Next, in the days that follow, when I connect with my trusted friends and loved ones, I tell them about my worst fears. Sharing in this way lessens my anxiety. I'm not sure why, but the relief and the strength I derive to move on purposefully is real.

Then I gather as much reliable data as I can about the problems that I might have to confront, (but not absolutely everything that Google has to offer), learning only as much as I need to develop a course of action for the present. I write it all down. Uncertainty is banished to another day, and my plan is available for rereading when it sneaks back in.

Len's Janis Ian

In the 1980's, my husband, Len, became aware of Janis Ian, a sing-
er-songwriter. He was captivated by her voice and the stories she
told in her songs. One by one her CDs appeared next to our stereo.

By this time our kids had all moved on to their adult lives, so the
choice of music in our home was what we alone favored. Len listened
to Ian's songs with an intensity I'd never before witnessed. If I was
present, I felt like an intruder. I walked into another room.

Soon he brought Ian tapes for the car, though he did not play them
when I was a passenger.

Rather than being drawn to listen and share her music, I was silently jealous of this woman who had so captivated my husband's attention. Did he fantasize having her in his life in some way?

I knew my reaction was absurd, and did not speak of it.

Then one day Len told me that he had written a letter to Ian to tell
her how moved he was by a particular song, (I don't know that he ever
mailed it, perhaps he did.) Momentarily, I felt a twinge akin to panic. I
said nothing, feeling too foolish. Or too vulnerable? Not sure. The
moment passed, only occasionally brought back to mind.

When Ian was not in the room, our loving ways were undisturbed.

On to part two of this story. Len died in 2002 bringing a close to
our fifty-three-year marriage. I knew our musician son, Grey, would
prize his music collection, so I suggested he take what he wished. He
took all of the Janis Ian CDs, which at that time were still tinged with
what I thought of as Len's yearning interest in this "other woman".

One morning a year or two after Len's death. I was snug in bed
reading the *Times*. I came upon an article beneath a picture of Janis
Ian and her partner, Pat, taken on their wedding day. Maybe you've
guessed, Pat is a woman, and the two of them had traveled to Canada
where same sex couples were allowed to marry.

I was filled with delight! How I wished that Len could have known.

And the story has another wonderful chapter. As part of his varied life as a musician, our son, Grey, was the music editor of the magazine, *Sing Out!*. He transcribed an Ian song for that publication. His work drew her attention, and she found it admirable and subsequently hired him to do all of the transcriptions for *Folk is the New Black*, her 2006 CD songbook. How overjoyed his father would have been to know of this connection.

CHAPTER SEVEN

MEN AND WOMEN

To Be a Man

When Father's Day approaches, a story I heard on the radio comes to mind. The question had been posed: "What does it mean to be manly today?" A listener in California called the station to address it.

The caller was a Mexican American who had come to this country at the age of seven, and was now in his thirties. He told of a family gathering with several generations in attendance. As evening approached, his wife rose and called to him across the room, "Honey, it's time to leave."

He joined her, and they said their goodbyes.

The next day his father disdainfully confronted him for allowing his wife to tell him when to leave. It was the man's place to make decisions, he reminded him, not to take orders from a woman.

In advance of the next family gathering, the caller asked his wife to silently signal him when she wished to go home. So on that occasion, as the evening waned, she glanced at him and arched her brows, and he announced that they must depart. His father smiled.

I love this story. The intimate complicity between husband and wife was just as it should be, preventing the inter-generational triangle from lessening the strength of their connection. For, even though the son was not willing to accept what was for him an outdated standard, he did not disparage his father's allegiance to his own code of conduct. Secure in his own manliness, the younger man had no need to return to adolescent push-back.

Over time the concept of manliness in my family shifted. My father and my husband, though of different generations, were similarly self-assured in their masculinity, gentle and respectful. They exercised no machismo, although both, when first married, assumed the traditional roles of their time.

At the time of my parents' marriage in 1922, my father pridefully insisted that his wife would never go to work (meaning: for money). My mother, who laughed as she told this story, said she ignored this edict, already having been the sole support of her widowed mother for a number of years. And once the Depression hit, the point was moot, and my father ignored it as well.

Len and I, married even before our college graduation in 1951, were members of the post-war "silent generation." He began graduate school, while I zealously embarked on my first career: motherhood. Our division of responsibility was unexamined and unremarkable, as he prepared to become the breadwinner and I the family caretaker. Then the tide turned, and in the 1960s I attended law school three nights a week for four years. On those evenings, Len would return from work at day's end to feed and bathe our three young children and put them to bed.

Was he exhibiting his feminine side? Actually, that's not how we thought of it. He was just helping out. We didn't characterize these tasks as unmanly. Nor do most men today, and the constraints of sexual stereotypes continue to loosen.

In later life, Len was grateful for having been cast into the richness of the caretaker role, often commenting to friends, "The women's movement was the best thing that ever happened to men."

Apology: Remorse Or Maneuver?

Apologies fill the air.
Professional crisis managers consult with counsel before drafting an equivocal response for the politician or corporate icon most recently exposed. We may groan, yet we understand the importance of considering future liability, criminal or civil. But what about our personal day-to-day interactions when we know we've contributed to hurt feelings or a misunderstanding? Is a defensive posture still called for?

I think back to a mediation client who phoned after a session and politely but firmly accused me of favoring a plan put forward by his wife, of displaying bias, not the neutrality I'd promised.

Although I thought his perception wrong, I knew I had likely contributed to this misunderstanding, so I simply apologized and said, "I am so sorry." That seemed to clear the air, and we were then able to listen to each other's view of what had taken place. Defensiveness fell away, for both of us.

But it could have gone quite differently, for I almost responded mindlessly, and defensively, by saying: "I'm sorry you see it that way."

I didn't say that, because of my heightened awareness of other expressions of regret gone awry. A celebrity or other contrite person of influence who, with great apparent sincerity, apologizes by saying, "If my words resulted in discomfort or pain, I'm very sorry." The speaker thereby shifts responsibility away from him or herself and onto the listener, who is presumed to be overly sensitive. Sincere remorse is not forthcoming. It's not really an apology at all.

Meeting with people who have hurt each other in egregious ways and decided to divorce, I did not often hear an apology spoken. When the decision was made to part, and anxiety about the future high, perhaps this is not surprising. But even under less stressful circumstances, in secure times, some can say they are sorry with ease, perhaps even be too apologetic, while others never utter the words of regret.

Deborah Tannen, a linguist, author and professor at Georgetown University, has written a number of books pointing out the differences between the communication style of most men and women, differences which she observed even in nursery school children at play. She notes that women often are willing to apologize when things have not worked out well. I've noticed that myself and assumed it simply grew out of women's greater ability to express feelings, and the reluctance of many men to display emotion. But, according to Tannen, there is more to it than that.

Women, she observes, tend to focus more on the question, "Is this conversation bringing us closer or pushing us further apart?" Men, on the other hand, tend to focus more on the question, "Is this conversation putting me in a one-up or one-down position?" She concludes that women tend to embrace apologies because apologies reinforce connections, while many men avoid them because of their symbolic power to advertise defeat.

More recent research, conducted by Carol Kinsey Gorman on gender differences in the workplace, suggests that there is little evidence to support this stereotype. Women do indeed resort to making more apologies than men, she agrees, but not because of men's fragile egos, but rather that men have a higher threshold for what constitutes offensive behavior. In the study, men rated imaginary or remembered offenses as less severe than women did. Perhaps both conclusions present meaningful distinctions, although they should be applied fully recognizing that generalizations don't always fit.

Putting gender differences aside, no doubt we all recognize that when we do something that harms someone else, a powerful new factor comes into play: the need to justify what we did. Can respect for the dignity of the other person overcome that need? I think so.

Unqualified expressions of remorse that take responsibility for acts or omissions are healing and open the door to understanding.

Nature Or Nurture?

Gloria Steinem, the ever-engaging feminist now in her eighties, challenged my generation to wake up and open doors long closed to women.

In June 2007, Steinem was the commencement speaker at Smith College, her Ivy League alma mater.

In my generation, [she said] we were asked by the Smith vocational office how many words we could type a minute, a question that was never asked of then all-male students at Harvard or Princeton. Female-only typing was rationalized by supposedly greater female verbal skills, attention to detail, smaller fingers, goodness knows what, but the public imagination just didn't include male typists, certainly not Ivy League-educated ones. Now computers have come along, and "typing" is "keyboarding." Suddenly, voila!---men can type! Gives you faith in men's ability to change, doesn't it?

What a hoot! So, we're all alike after all. But, apparently we're not.

For the past thirty years, feminists (I among them) insisted that socialization alone is determinative of men's and women's skill development and therefore choice of career. If someone suggests that a biological or genetic trait differentiates the intellectual capabilities of men and women, they are pilloried. Witness the long slide of Lawrence Summers, from the pinnacle of Harvard's presidency, when he suggested that women might be less well suited for scientific endeavor. A furor ensued. A resignation. Thoughtful responses were hushed.

Yet today even parents committed to raising children free of sexual stereotypes describe the differences they witness between their young sons and daughters as very real, almost from infancy. They buy their two-year-old girls trucks and fire engines, and they still drift to playing house. They allow, even encourage, their young boys to play with dolls, but they still end up pointing their G.I. Joes at each other simulating gunfire.

Socialization? Well, maybe.

Enter brain imaging and other advanced explorations of the human body. Prenatal exposure to differing levels of hormones is currently of great interest to the many researchers who are seriously asking why aren't more women in science?* Males appear to have superiority in spatial reasoning, while women have a greater talent for language.

As one of only two women in my 1969 law school graduating class of 44, it's easy to stand on the nurture side of the line, but I think we need to wait and see and take a less defensive stance, as we watch the balance between biologically preordained and socially imposed characteristics play out.

I hope we continue to recognize and question institutional bias in hiring and promotion, but let's also welcome the inquiry and refrain from demonizing the messenger

*Why Aren't More Women in Science? Top Researchers Debate the Evidence by Wendy M. Williams (author), Stephen J. Ceci (editor).

Trusting Snap Decisions

The conventional wisdom, when you are faced with an important decision, is to consider the pros and cons. Sometimes I do that, perhaps just in thought, or I write a list. But, most often, by the time I get around to taking this deliberate approach, I already know what my decision will be, or at least what my more impulsive self yearns to do. Then, having made the decision, occasionally I question the lack of serious attention given to the more analytical process.

At nineteen, I decided to marry Len. (We married young in those days.) In the late 1950s, we decided on a house to buy. In the mid-1960s I decided to go to law school. In the 1980s, I decided to transition from a litigation-based practice to less lucrative work as a mediator. These were all major decisions, and I made each of them almost in the blink of an eye, well in advance of any systematic analysis.

In his book *Blink*, Malcolm Gladwell describes our ability to make quick judgments based on our past experiences. This "instant processing," as he calls it, accurately serves as a sound guide for decision making. As human beings, he maintains, we are capable of making sense of situations based on the thinnest slice of experience---"the power of thin-slicing." His premise is detailed and well researched, offered with the emphatic caveat that when we make a quick decision based on erroneous data (i.e. unexamined prejudices), the results are often disastrous.

The day I first met Len, all those years ago, we went for a walk in the woods that bordered our college campus. There we came upon two newborn rabbits, eyes not yet open. Their mother had been killed by a predator. Len rescued these little bits of wildlife, nestling them on a soft cloth crumpled into an old cigar box.

To this day, a small black and white photo of the tiny rabbits stands on my desk. A hand, large in comparison to the tiny creatures, holds the box. Next to it is a small beaker of milk with an eyedropper.

To those who ask about the photo, I explain that it was taken the day I met Len, and the hand is his.

I never examined the reason why I keep the picture close by, but Gladwell's book helped me figure it out. The young man tenderly caring for orphaned rabbit babies was a kind and compassionate person. We were drawn to each other, no doubt making other snap judgments along the way. We married two years later. The very significant differences in our backgrounds suggested to many that our decision was unwise. But we never added up the pros and cons, and gave little heed to the caution of others--- happily so.

The Price Of Incivility: Who Pays?

I'm a devotee of contemporary fiction, but I've been revisiting Jane Austen, returning through the exquisite prose of *Pride and Prejudice* to a society devoted to and even obsessed with social etiquette. It serves as a welcome respite from some modern media that jars my sensibilities.

This sharp contrast between Austen's genial spoken exchanges and the offhand and sometimes crude phrases of today came to mind when someone suggested I write about civility in the legal profession, so often said to be in decline. I was reluctant: as a woman of a certain age, I questioned whether my observations would have validity for men, or for younger women raised with the same assurance afforded sons that the world is potentially their oyster and that they can have it on their own terms.

And I wondered whether the decline in civility really matters? It might be upsetting for those of us with expectations born of past sensibility, or mythology. But perhaps our shifting social mores and the broad acceptance of a more candid and direct way of speaking is simply benign evidence of a new, less mannerly age?

I remembered those times in my legal practice when someone talked to me rudely or disrespectfully, when an overly aggressive or insensitive rejoinder would throw me off balance. These experiences left me feeling exposed, embarrassed, and possibly even shamed.

In the late 1960s, when I was a law student, I sat in the conference room of a prominent firm, surrounded by a five-man committee charged with determining if law students were fit to be candidates for the bar exam. I'd previously written and submitted my essay on why I chose law as a profession. A well-known attorney seated at the head of the table had my file open before him. He held it up and said, "Hubby write this for you?"

My quiet response: "No."

Fast forward. A novice at the bar, I stood before a Judge who was known to be mean-spirited. I had negotiated a plea bargain for my client, who was present for sentencing. In a calm strong voice, I put forth his better qualities, the sound reasons for his release on probation. The judge smiled down at me. "So, counsel," he said, "if he's such a fine fellow, I suggest you take him home with you." I was speechless, embarrassed for him and for myself.

A third instance took place in the late 1970s, again before the bench. This time the judge was a kind elderly man who nodded and smiled as he listened to my motion argument. I was then director of the Public Defender Office. Said the Judge, "I'll take this under advisement, but send Annie T. down to represent this fellow, and have her wear that red sweater."

I blushed and said nothing. Laughter erupted in the courtroom.

And in a more current incident, I sat across the desk from opposing counsel to discuss the complex valuation issues in a difficult divorce case. My presentation was detailed, carefully researched and well reasoned. My adversary announced, "This is completely ridiculous, ludicrous!"

Did I calmly ask for his reasons? No, again I was momentarily silenced. And when I did respond, I'd lost my focus.

So, what happens when incivility is in the room?

Lest the reader conclude that it is only sexism at play here, many times as a mediator I've witnessed men respond to a belligerent comment, sarcasm, or threat. First he abruptly snaps shut the briefcase, and then he rises from his chair, saying, "Fine! I'll see you in Court." Even if I somehow bar the door and keep the conversation going, the mood in the room has changed, darkened. Muscles are tensed, and positions hardened.

Happily, my personal incidents of incivility have been few, although the memories are vivid. Note that these were not comments about something I had done, or to correct a mistake of fact or judgment, but about who I was.

The underlying message of the offensive words, whether they are aggressive, insults or insidious innuendos, is: You are not worthy of my respect. Sometimes artfully disguised behind a congenial smile, they penetrate the boundaries with which we protect our unique private vulnerabilities, the delicate balance we maintain in every adversarial or unequal setting.

Civility welcomes what is best in me, without my needing the protective armor that blocks intelligent intercourse. The offender, the bully, may really be the fearful one, his verbal thrust of apparent strength a way of hiding his weakness. Or his sarcasm may be an attempt to divert others from his inability to address the issues.

Faced with incivility, we feel attacked and the fight-or-flight or freeze reaction takes over. Neither response is conducive to reasoned progress being made on a client's behalf.

That's who really pays the price.

Threatened By Fantasy

I wish I could think and write more intelligently about adult pornography. The very word looms large on the page or when spoken, and is rarely mentioned in mixed company, even among good friends. Some well-known women academics regard it as an unmitigated evil, but the very existence of an industry that draws in many billions of dollars a year reflects a demand these authors do not address, except to seek censorship. Does prohibition ever work?

Admittedly, my vantage point is narrow. The few porn films I've actually seen, I found seriously wanting, offering no context that would provide women, at least, with any sustainable interest.

In the 1970s, my public defender years, the courthouse was my bailiwick. From the sidelines, I followed the criminal trials of the producers of pornographic films (after all, we do know it when we see it), some of them notorious. Eventually, as juries began to return not-guilty verdicts, prosecutions dwindled, and in 1975 the VCR arrived in the marketplace and theatergoers retreated into the seclusion of their homes. The shift to the Internet offers viewers even greater privacy, until discovered.

Pornography entered my professional world when some wives in mediation told about their husband's Internet exploration, calling it a factor contributing to the disintegration of their marriage. But was it a cause or an effect? Remembering their stories, I still don't know.

What is clear is that for some women, a partner's interest becomes a defining issue. They are convinced that their partner's vivid fantasy life weakens the marriage bond, as it seems to call into question their own desirability. Unable to talk about it, the intimate dance that brought them together goes into reverse, and she withdraws to a self-imposed isolation. If he had reassured her of her desirability, would the outcome have been different?

For some, the issue is a moral one. Their upbringing or religious belief affords them absolute clarity of judgment, allowing for no accommodation. Their partner must respect their position, even if they do not share it. But for many, their partner's clandestine and solitary involvement evokes concern that it creates a yearning that erodes commitment. Is that true? Is that inevitable?

Because open discussion of this taboo subject is rare, I have little knowledge of those couples who successfully address the issue with a counselor, or those where the viewer's interest is not condemned, may even be joined, or simply treated lightly, tolerated, or just ignored.

In mediation, my conversations with the husbands, the accused watchers, are typically brief and superficial. They've been "outed", are somewhat embarrassed, but neither deny their interest nor make excuses. In all respects known to me, they are honorable and healthy men, supporting their families, devoted to their children. Their exterior life in the community is openly on display, while their interior fantasy life allows them to secretly travel wherever they wish. Or it did until now, when their wives meet them with rage or sullen silence, or accuse them of perversity, and their families fall apart.

About more familiar fantasies, I can think and write intelligently. There is probably not a married person alive who has not, at least in their interior life, envisioned the "what ifs?" What if I'd married someone else? What if we separated or divorced? What if ten years from now I regret missing important opportunities? What if I seek a major change in my life right now and give it primacy over the accepted patterns in my marriage?

I remember times when "what ifs?" were on my mind, and times I imagined my husband asking himself similar questions. Some of those moments were scary.

But those daydreams turned out to be healthy, even if they were unsettling. For eventually we talked. They provoked change, urging small steps that gently shifted our established ways, or even major moves that altered life's course.

We honor "what if" speculations, whether they are enticing or frightening, whether they are about intimacy, a job change or even global disaster. One day, comfortable doing so, a conversation can begin. Is that also possible in the realm of explicit, deceptively idealized sexuality?

Is porn inevitably destructive? May it also bring important questions into the open? If, rather than passing unwavering judgment, could a more nuanced discussion be had? Without assigning blame, might changes then be made to improve upon the reality, the fantasy world accepted as just that?

Or is that a fantasy?

Some Beliefs To Reconsider

Never a fan of televised sporting events, there was a time in my past that I pretended to be, as a way of sharing cozy moments with my husband. I wasn't a complete fraud. I could get caught up in the ballet of basketball or the graceful beauty of skiing and skating.

But although I found football a bore, I loved watching the post touchdown hugging, and even the congratulatory slap on the rump.

Women usually embrace when they greet each other in a social setting, while most men show greater reserve and shake hands. Seeing men lose their restraint with other men, joyously sharing a celebratory bond, was heartwarming. Sporting events used to be the only time I witnessed this, except among close family members. In many families, the male embrace, even between fathers and sons, remains awkward or absent.

Just before President George W. Bush addressed a joint session of Congress in 2001, in the televised view of millions, he exchanged bear hugs with both Senator Tom Daschle and Representative Dick Gephardt. Those hugs were worthy of comment on the front page of *The New York Times* the next day. Back then, men hugging in public outside of the sports arena was still remarkable.

But over recent decades, this stereotype that women are more physically expressive in a joyous moment has begun to fade.

Other gender stereotypes have also fallen by the wayside. Here are some I now often witness:

Over the last forty years, as more and more women entered the workplace, many men began to significantly share the care of infants and young children. Over time they found the role of nurturer as natural and rewarding as women have. These fathers model for their sons and daughters that men and women alike can provide tenderness and comfort.

When couples divorce, women who have the higher income are no happier paying alimony than most men ever were. Those who've accumulated larger pension funds than their divorcing husbands often fail to see the fairness in having to share them with their spouse. They are likely to use the exact same rationale so often previously expressed by men: "I'm the one who worked so hard to earn it, surely it is mine alone to keep." Clearly, economic savvy and self-interest are not gender specific.

Women entering scientific fields so long dominated by men are proving, just as those who entered the legal profession have done, that they are as capable as their male counterparts. Whether women are equally comfortable in this competitive arena is far less clear. I think not yet.

How often do we thoughtlessly accept, even act upon, stereotypes distinguishing the supposed characteristics of men and women, the generalizations we grew up with that men are more analytical and less emotional, while women are more nurturing, more intuitive? Scientists are now bent upon identifying those sectors of the brain that light up to display different functions, and I leave it to them to catalog the impact of male and female hormones on behavior. For now, our assumptions bear re-examination.

I hope that women, as we continue to break through the glass ceiling and become more politically visible, don't diminish the importance of being expressive and fostering intimate relationships. So much better, from my perspective, for it to work just the other way around, so that men become more comfortable expressing their feelings and loosening their hold on cool reserve.

A Missed Opportunity

A former high school classmate recently died. In honor of his re-markable life, I and three other old friends of his spoke to an audience of young people now attending the same school. Looking back on that occasion, I realize I missed an important opportunity.

As the only woman on the panel, I decided to comment on how the aspirations of boys and girls differed when I was in high school in the 1940s. I would also pay homage to two of my high school teachers who caused me to wonder whether my future was actually as limited as I then assumed it was.

The men on the panel---a doctor, a lawyer and an architect---all had made major contributions to the public good. From their earliest days, they could answer the ubiquitous question: *And what are you going to be when you grow up?* Perhaps when very young, they said *fireman* or *policeman*. Was I ever asked the question, or was there no need to ask a little girl? But had I been asked as I entered my teen years, what might I have answered: *teacher? nurse?* And, of course: *wife and mother*. But in their teen years, these boys would likely have said, *doctor, lawyer* or *architect*. We looked at our place in the world differently. When young, I knew no women who were doctors, law-yers, or architects.

The message I received from my parents and the world around me in those pre-college years was clear:

*Be smart and get a good education, for you may have to support your family if your husband dies or falls ill.

*Be good (which meant no sex before marriage).

*Be pretty, and don't act too smart, so you can attract the right man and marry by twenty.

These early messages were not easily discarded, and I did marry at twenty. In my mid-thirties, as the mother of three, I was swept along by the 1960s women's movement and entered law school. But when quizzed by friends about how I would use a law degree, this Perry Mason devotee responded, "Well, if I were a man, I would practice criminal law."

I told this personal story to my young audience. Was it meaningful as anything other than a history lesson? Do girls today see themselves standing on equal footing with their brothers? Is the message now the same for sons and daughters?

*Be smart and get a good education.

*Practice safe sex.

*Attractive people get ahead faster and go further in life.

With hindsight, I missed an opportunity to pose some important questions:

Are young people today contemplating how, in the years to come, they will balance a career with raising children? Are they thinking through and talking and talking some more to their future life-partner about the parenting role each will play?

Are they reading the stories that glorify women who've decided to abandon careers and stay home to raise their families? And do they then ask themselves what if...? And do they know the less frequently told stories about women, more numerous by far, who are left to essentially raise children on their own?

Perhaps this was not the occasion for me to pose these questions, yet I regret not doing so. I hope someone is asking them whether being on equal footing in their teens carries a promise of balanced lives when children arrive.

And not asking the girls alone.

CHAPTER EIGHT

SELF DISCLOSURE

The Gift Of Self Disclosure

The message left on my phone: *Could you find time for an early breakfast? I need some legal advice.*

From the tremor in the voice of my young friend, Carole, I could tell that something was wrong. We met the next morning, and without preamble she told me that her husband had suffered a mental breakdown. This man she dearly loved had become a stranger to her and was refusing treatment. Frightened by his mood swings and bizarre accusations, she had left him and moved into the home of a colleague from work. We discussed her options, personal and legal. The nervous movements of her hands belied her effort to appear calm.

I asked whether she had talked things over with a counselor, or her friends, or her parents and siblings, who lived some distance away. She had not and urged me to keep her confidence. Hoping that somehow this nightmare would reverse itself and all would be set right again, she was protecting the privacy of her marriage and avoiding the embarrassment of disclosure. Nor did she want to worry her family before her future plans were clear.

It was understandable, but I gently questioned her choice to put off sharing this difficult time with trusted friends and family. Couldn't she even express uncertainty about what lay ahead? An insightful person, she confessed that her silence was in large part a way of avoiding revealing something that seemed shameful: The nature of his illness and her desertion of him.

Her tears reminded me of times I'd kept my own past secrets too long before the telling.

Many years ago, I told her, my friend, Dona, had been diagnosed with breast cancer. That was back when cancer still carried a stigma and was often borne in silence. Within hours of receiving the diagnosis, she told all her friends and family. I remember being surprised, suspecting that I would have done just the opposite, telling no one until it became impossible not to do so.

But I learned a lesson from her reaction, for upon hearing her news, many people rallied around her, expressing concern and support. That outpouring of loving attention buoyed her sense of well-being. Openly telling people about her illness brought her the comfort of connection with others, dispelling the loneliness of hidden fears.

Carole nodded as she listened, even showed a faint smile, but remained worried as she imagined the reaction to her news. She promised to call again in a day or so, and to consider meeting with a therapist.

The marvelous truth is that by disclosing ourselves to close friends and loved ones, we not only secure their support, we invite them to be equally revealing. Quite literally, being able to share the bad news as well as the good is a gift, sending the message to others that we will be there for them when it is their story that needs to be told.

Taking To The Sky

W hen my husband was in his late forties, he learned to pilot a small plane, and he fell in love.

When the weather was good, he wanted to fly. When the weather was poor, but not too poor, he wanted to test his mettle. When it was dark, he wanted to practice night flying. Flying became his passion. And he wanted to share it with me.

Covertly, I was an anxious passenger. The noise of the engine and the crackle of the radio precluded conversation. Ever vigilant lest we collide with other aircraft, I couldn't fathom what kept us aloft. I felt like I was in the Warner Brothers cartoon where the coyote races toward the edge of a cliff and then keeps right on running in thin air, only to suddenly look down and drop like a stone (and bounce).

Len's patient instruction about the principle of airfoils didn't help.

Yet for several years I flew with him, even making two cross-country trips. He was in his element. Upon landing, I was always so happy to be back on firm ground that this was the emotion he noted. But my dread could not be kept secret.

I consulted a psychologist who specialized in desensitization of phobias, for that was how my fear was defined. At the second session, she asked how often I flew with Len. Three or four times a week, I said, Surprised and puzzled, she asked why I went so often if I didn't enjoy it?

Aha! This was the critical question and a defining moment. We changed course and focused on exploring what other fears I was keeping hidden. It turned out that I was afraid of not living up to my concept of what a good wife should be, and of being abandoned as unworthy.

I'd like to report that recognizing those fears erased my fear of flying in a small plane, but it didn't.

Instead, I decided to give up flying with Len altogether. A good solution for me, less so for him. I was relaxed enough to tell him without undue guilt. He expressed sincere disappointment. Fair enough---we were both entitled to be authentic.

Thereafter he found many enthusiastic flying companions---fishing buddies, geology graduate students. Eventually our teenage daughter and his then seventy-three-year-old mother accompanied him on a trip to explore Alaska by plane, fulfilling a boyhood dream.

Did he express regret from time to time, about my not being his companion on some exciting adventure? Yes, and that made me sad for a while. Sometimes old feelings of insecurity returned, but they didn't last long.

And if anything, honesty drew us closer.

An Unquiet Mind

Can simply reading another's personal history significantly impact our own?

Kay Redfield Jamison's book *An Unquiet Mind* was given to me by a friend when I confided that a member of my extended family was exhibiting extreme behaviors. I'd begun to wonder whether I was witnessing the normal range of craziness that accompanies the breakup of a marriage, or a serious mood disorder, perhaps of long standing.

Jamison, a psychologist on the faculty of Johns Hopkins Medical School, is an expert on manic-depressive illness. The remarkable twist in her story is that she has suffered with this disorder since her late teens, though not diagnosed or treated for many years thereafter.

Publication of this revealing memoir in 1995 was made by a woman who had previously gone to great lengths to conceal her condition, knowing exposure would likely sidetrack her career. Then, at some considerable cost, she surrendered her privacy. Although as a tenured professor, "outing" herself was less risky than it might have been, writing about being psychotic and delusional did cause some of her generally supportive colleagues to treat her differently and question her motivation and objectivity. But not for long.

Her book, expected to draw a limited audience, remained on bestseller lists for five months and soon sold over 400,000 copies, proving what great hunger there is for understanding when a loved one goes off the rails, and the ripple effect of mental illness. Others sought insight to their own troubling behaviors.

Jamison describes a time when although medicated, she was within the throes of the dreadful agitation of a manic state. Her work required she back away from these feelings to focus on analyzing research data she was preparing for a publication deadline. She needed to gain control over her irrational distorted thoughts.

These words describing her effort had special meaning for me: "Much as I had done when frightened or upset as a child, I found that asking questions, tracking down answers as best I could, and then asking yet more questions was the best way to provide a distance from anxiety and a framework for understanding."

Jamison's method can be a prescription for us all. Even those spared the devastation of mental illness fall into periods of mild or moderate depression and anxiety. For me too, asking myself the right questions, and in this way becoming more self-aware, allays anxiety

At this advanced stage of life, I've figured out which questions to ask, to manage those emotions which otherwise sweep away rational thought, when faced with anxiety or mild depression and awake and unable to regain sleep at 3:00 am.

I take paper and pen in hand and write down the following questions and the answers that flow:

What are the recent troubling events now on my mind (i.e. report of an adult child's illness, rejection of a friendly overture, a professional misstep)?

What emotions have been triggered (i.e. anxiety, sadness, anger, shame)?

What thoughts about my life are generated by those events and emotions (i.e. I'm helpless, unloved, irresponsible, unworthy)?

In what way are these thoughts irrational or distorted (i.e. all or nothing reasoning, predicting the future without sufficient evidence, plagued by old scripts of "shoulds" and "oughts"), categories so well explained and defined by my reading and study of Cognitive Behavioral Therapy (CBT)?

What rational thoughts could replace those that are distorted and generate my anxiety or mild depression? (If having difficulty at this stage, I ask myself this question: If a dear friend brought this narrative to my door, what advice would I offer? The ideas then flow.)

Then, my writings are set aside for review in the morning, and with thanks to Kay Redfield Jamison, I go back to sleep.

Talking Things Over

I'm trying to make a difficult decision, lying awake for hours at night. But as I share my concern with close friends, some calm begins to return.

Long ago this became my way of coping when troubles arose, but it calls for a measure of self-disclosure, a sharing of vulnerabilities, which I know is hard for some.

A while ago an old friend began phoning more often than usual. Her son was divorcing, and her distress about the breakup of his family had brought her low. She had been my frequent talking partner when angst was in my life, so now it was my turn to listen.

My husband and I had lived through a similar time, when a child's divorce became part of the air we breathed, often the last thing we talked about at night and the first upon waking. But when I say we talked about it, that's not quite true. I talked, he listened. For longer conversations, I turned to my friend.

One evening, overhearing us on the phone, Len gently berated me, urging me to think and talk less about the plight of our loved ones. He saw it as a way of quieting my concerns. I did not argue with him but simply ignored his advice, as he knew I would.

Len grew up in a home where feelings, even if recognized, were not talked about. In my childhood home, emotion was welcome grist for the mill. Not surprisingly, we both grew up having adopted the ways we learned as children. He was able to put troubles out of mind and metaphorically go fishing. Not me.

We knew this about each other. Over time, and with deliberate effort, talk came more easily for us, but we also learned to honor our differences. I probed less to unearth the feelings behind his moods, and he sought less to divert or dampen my need to talk when I was upset. When we were not in sync for conversation, a comforting touch or a loving embrace allowed us to communicate without words. Today my friends, those who talk and those who mostly listen, fill the void.

A colleague, who is also a close friend, listens well, offering comfort when things go amiss in my life or when I'm faced with a challenging decision. She has suffered major losses and faced difficult choices, but she rarely discloses her most personal thoughts. Although I know she trusts me, she keeps her feelings hidden beneath an exterior of cheerful banter. She willingly talks of her professional life and the problems she is working to solve for her clients, but when her friends inquire about her well-being, she just gives a few reassuring words, then artfully changes the subject. Efforts to thwart this move inevitably fail.

I find this worrisome. Did her family meet distress with silence, and she now follows the avoidance pattern of her early years? I try to respect the line she has drawn. But I'm sad for her and wonder when a self-imposed barrier becomes a cage, even a prison.

Does our personal past inform our professional present? Lawyers, by the very nature of their work, hear from clients when they are most vulnerable. They usually respect personal boundaries, appropriately so. But over the years I've grown less guarded. On occasion I step cautiously into that protected space of professional reserve and share with a client a story of a similar experience to theirs, or one from which I learned something important. Lightning does not strike. My status is not compromised. A sweet connection is made.

For years I've kept a wonderful Edward Koren cartoon on my desk. It shows two couples enjoying a companionable evening in the living room of one of them. Behind the host couple, who are seated on their couch, stands a huge hairy monster. "We deal with it by talking about it" reads the caption.

I do too, and I count myself lucky to know others for whom demons are diminished by talk, even if sometimes they just listen.

Out Of Sync

Sometimes partners drift apart slowly and move into separate worlds, failing to disclose to each other the person they're evolving to become. They may be communicating in subtle nonverbal ways, but is the message getting through?

John and Mary have similar backgrounds and compatible values. When their children were small, they delighted in being parents and assigned themselves the traditional roles of breadwinner and homemaker. As years went by, John, a gregarious man, was increasingly successful in business and developed close friendships in that world. While he spent more and more hours at work, Mary found satisfaction and pleasure in her focus on their daughters, now teenagers.

Then he became quiet and more withdrawn at home. She asked if everything was all right, knowing it wasn't. He had stopped going to the gym and was putting on excessive weight. But his answers were vague, and she chose to interpret his equivocation as stress at work. So she backed away to "give him the space he seemed to need." They were out of sync, and over the next several years, they gradually moved apart, both dissatisfied but neither saying much that was to the point.

John's physician referred him to a psychiatrist who prescribed antidepressants. They helped his mood but not his ability or willingness to share his feelings with his wife. Within months he suggested divorce. How could she have been surprised? But she was.

As their mediator, I concentrate on the decisions they must make about their future, so I ask few questions about their past. I gain just a superficial knowledge of their personal dynamic and little of their early formative years. I listen well, but their messages are often delivered in code.

"We used to do things together," John says, "although all the planning was left up to me. I have to initiate everything, and half the time

she has no interest in my suggestions, seems more involved in the social lives of our girls."

"He had no time for us," Mary says. "He didn't even come to
school performances." She showed me a picture of their attractive
daughters, in provocative dress and stance.

My unspoken questions: *Is he saying Mary no longer finds him de-
sirable? Is she saying the day of her attractiveness has passed and
now belongs to her daughters?*

Many midlife parents, in different ways, experience discomfort
with the emerging sexuality of their children. These are stressful times
when divorce rates climb. Was that the case with John and Mary?

I can only make an intelligent guess, and it may be way off base.
But my guess doesn't really matter.

The tragedy is that John and Mary too were only able to guess, but
that really does matter to them. They lack the skill to be self-
disclosing with each other---about this they now agree. So, did their
feelings of discomfort, rejection, or inadequacy remain hidden? While
still sharing a bed, did they become strangers?

If both partners are unable to verbalize their feelings or intuit those
of the other, we do not have much reason to be hopeful about their
future. If even one has the emotional intelligence to express their feelings and draw the other into a non-blaming conversation, there would
be some reason to be hopeful.

But if both partners were motivated and felt safe enough to talk
openly about their desires and disappointments, and early on to enlist
the aid of a skilled professional, they might get the prize: An intact
family.

Truth Telling

You are trying to decide whether to disclose an important truth, but reconsider when a friend urges caution and suggests that you not take the unnecessary risk. So you reconsider. You decide to postpone the decision, even as you yearn for the release that authenticity would bring. You are stalled by ambivalence.

We grow up being told to always tell the truth. But parents inevitably send a more nuanced message when we hear them tell a half-truth, or tell untruths out of kindness, or remain silent, perhaps to keep a promised confidence, and thereby send a false message.

Is it better to tell or not tell?

I am sometimes asked this question by a partner who has strayed and now seeks to revive a relationship gone adrift, or who wishes to avoid the consequences of an angry response. I have no pat answer. The complexity of people's lives, which even good fiends know only partially, suggests that giving advice on this issue would be unwise. At best, we can suggest probing questions for the keeper of the secret to explore. Sometimes it seems that making the admission will well serve only the teller, not the unknowing other. Guilt is made more bearable by confession.

But others find living with deception to be untenable, believing that only through a shared honest exploration of the past, and the hoped-for future, can they restore or possibly transform a genuinely loving and committed relationship. Disclosure offers both parties the opportunity to explore new choices and take new directions. Holding on to the secret denies the unknowing party the chance to consider a different path.

It's risky, either way. And it's not an easy call when the decision to tell the truth is unilateral, but the impact of truth-telling potentially falls on many.

A case in point: for some time, a wife has been silently enduring her husband's sustained lack of sexual interest. Finally she gathers the strength to ask him if he is gay. He answers emphatically and angrily that he is not--- knowing that he is. He fears that exposure will cause the loss of his precious connection with his young children.

I was asked for advice about this potential disclosure, and I surprised even myself by comfortably responding, "Of course, the truth should be told." And in this case, it was. All his worst fears came true in living color. His wife raged. He was awash in guilt and dread. The children were confused and frightened, and the family's community of friends were unbelieving, some falling away. The family shed many tears and endured sleepless nights. But over time, with the support of skilled professionals and loyal friends, the family was reconfigured, and acceptance and accommodation evolved. They once again expressed loving feelings. The world shifted, but righted.

This truth clearly had to be told, for the damaging impact of keeping the secret seemed too serious to justify the lack of honest disclosure. But *clearly* is not a good choice of words, for these decisions are often anything but clear. Had this wife been a vengeful, vindictive person, her gay husband might well have made a different choice or at least postponed the truth telling.

Not long ago I confided to a colleague, a young female attorney, that I still have occasional moments of self-doubt and that fears of poor performance can bring on a blue mood. Weeks later when we met again, her eyes brimmed with tears as she shared her gratitude. How reassuring it was, she told me, to know that such feelings, which sometimes haunted her days, were not hers alone, but were shared by someone who had already achieved significant professional success. What a gratifying moment for me, for both of us. Disclosure begets disclosure.

On reaching adulthood and beyond, as self-knowledge and self-acceptance grow, most of us allow ourselves a good measure of authenticity, a willingness to openly share our truths. One of the true joys of growing old is recognizing that the need for pretense falls away. And that one is loved nonetheless, even admired, for sharing truths that it once seemed important to hide.

But concerns will inevitably still arise when we must choose between telling a hard truth and protecting our privacy. We strive to maintain the delicate balance between our own well-being and possible harm to others. Perhaps that effort is one important definition of maturity.

The Shame Of Illness

I have few memories of illness in my family as I was growing up. My parents barely acknowledged minor ailments. They spoke of sickness as something that, with proper living, could be avoided. They often deemed the illness of others psychosomatic, not without sympathy, but with an underlying message of some hidden weakness that should be overcome.

In my husband Len's final year, I became intimately involved with persistent pain. He was stoic, but when he left the house for an adventure with a friend, I would assist in placing the Parkinson's meds he needed to take at set times in a small pocket container. I noticed when the number of tablets he added for pain relief increased. It made me uneasy.

During our regular visits to physicians, the initial question was often, "On a scale of one to ten, how's the pain?" Len might answer, "Nine." Compression fractures in his spine were the apparent cause, but I was dismayed and embarrassed by his admission.

I've read that many people are ashamed to talk about pain, whether it be a passing headache or something more chronic. But those who make the effort to describe their pain in some detail, a study found, were better able to cope with the pain thereafter.

I suspect this relates to emotional pain as well.

Some time ago, I had a scare, arising from a routine physical. My doctor ordered an ultrasound, then an MRI. Then, of course, I spent a week waiting for results.

I made the decision to share this information with no one, rationalizing that any disclosure would be premature. But my inner turmoil belied this determination, and when a close colleague asked why I seemed so distracted, my story poured forth. The next day I told other intimate friends. That evening I emailed my kids, giving them the details.

The reduction in stress was palpable.

Soon the reassuring news came that all was well.

Why the initial reluctance to tell anyone? Was I shamed by an old parental message that illness was in some way a punishment for wrongdoing? What better defense mechanism could I have than to hide this presumably moral flaw of not being the person Mother wanted me to be?

Well, there is bound to be a next time. I hope my recent experience will finally silence my childhood script that illness is somehow shameful and to be denied. Unexpressed fears, and pain, can loom larger than life. Giving voice to them not only opens the way to receive loving support but lightens the step and makes it easier to breathe.

How Dare You Ask?

A fable: On a lovely fall day, Jan and Joe drove away from the city, admiring the leaves turned crimson and gold. Their thoughts were on a soon-to-be-enjoyed romantic interlude at the Cozy Country Inn. They had been seeing each other for a few weeks, and the time seemed right for greater intimacy. Their instincts were true. Their liaison was passionate and satisfying.

The next morning, cheered by their new beginning, they entered the dining room feeling optimistic about their future. Over blueberry waffles they talked:

Jan: "So, tell me more about your job."

Joe: "You mean what do I do, day to day?"

Jan: "Well, what do you earn?"

Joe fell silent and raised his hands to his chest, palms outward in the universal gesture of: *back off.* They traveled home in silence.

An overreaction? Perhaps, but perhaps not.

Why is it so difficult, even with an intimate, to talk about money?

Except for close family, I have few friends with whom I talk freely about our finances, what we each earn and what we have accumulated. When I've inquired of others, most tell me that they have even fewer confidants for such talk, and some have none at all. Even family members are often kept essentially in the dark and know better than to ask. And if someone does ask, doubts arise.

What is the questioner's motive?

Will I be judged inadequate, unworthy?

Will I build a false expectation of largess?

If she earns more than I do, will I be diminished in her eyes?

We comfortably talk about the money of other people, often scoffing at those who've accumulated millions yet relentlessly strive for more. We ask: When is enough enough? Money doesn't buy happiness, or so we assure each other. But we do not turn to our conversation partner and ask about their finances, unwilling to risk undermining an ego, theirs or our own. Personal talk about money is the ultimate taboo.

Does what we earn or own define our intrinsic worth in the eyes of others? Is that the essential fear? Sharing in the exquisite privacy of the sexual realm is far easier, as we and our partner reassure each other of the potential for mutuality, and of our value to each other. But exposing our finances, revealing our ability to compete for dollars--- that is subjecting ourselves to judgment by the external standards of society. It means putting our ego strength in the hands of the fickle marketplace. So we hide.

The moral of the fable: The one who is gleefully stripped bare in the bedroom, in the counting room must be afforded ample cover.

CHAPTER NINE

NEGOTIATION

The Folly Of Giving Advice

I'm watching a young family self-destruct. I cast caution to the wind and offer some advice. A foolish move.

The story: Two young physicians have sought me out for mediation, to end their five-year marriage. They have built a reservoir of misery for themselves and for their child. After just one meeting, I think I know how they can avert disaster.

He is smart, charming, and articulate, qualities that had no doubt attracted her. But though soft spoken, he is a very angry man. Now that their marriage is almost over, his anger has taken center stage, sometimes covert and subtle, but often sharp and direct. She says it is what has driven her away and sees herself as the victim in their drama.

But when his verbal saber slices the air, thrusting, she parries. They are frozen in this dance, on the brink of waging legal warfare. Their child is young, so they will have many years ahead to play their roles.

My ego gets in the way of my wisdom, so in private I give him advice: "Get therapeutic help. Seek the source of your rage, and try to understand, and overcome it."

My advice to her: "With your ardent defensive reactions to his anger, you're turning control of your life over to the very man you're trying to escape. Get some help to figure out how you can change your responses. Don't live with the hope or expectation that you can best him at this game, or that he is the one who will change."

Neither acknowledges nor attends to what I urge upon them. Just the opposite. She pays no heed and changes the subject. He becomes resentful and withdraws. My advice may have been sound. Offering it was not.

I step back and examine my folly, and bring my failed experience to a thoughtful colleague. And she says: "You've stepped across a boundary and took on a role that is not yours to play. You can't change their lives with motivation that is yours, not theirs."

They're words I might have spoken to another, but did not speak to myself in my rush to rescue them. They had not come to me for salvation.

Good advice may be a great gift, but giving it in a constructive way is an art. My knowledge of this pair was superficial, their situation far more complex than it initially appeared. An empathic listening connection had barely begun. With only meager acquaintance, one cannot know what is best for someone else.

Even with close friends or family members, unsolicited personal advice is usually an unwelcome intrusion into another's life, suggesting that they are not capable of working out their own issues, a lack of due regard. In this circumstance, I should at least have asked whether my advice was wanted, and posed the question in a way that allowed for either a yes or no answer.

There are some things I can do in my role as mediator (not savior), or as a friend or family member, that might be helpful, and which I may still have the opportunity to do with my young clients. I could share my personal experiences in dealing with anger, my own, and in responding to that of another. This is information they could choose to make use of or ignore, but sharing it would not be a show of disrespect. And I can ask questions that would help them explore possible options going forward, so they can then consider the likely consequences of each path. This might take considerable time, but it would be time well spent.

In the end, wisely or not, we usually act on what we have come to believe is our best course of action, not on what someone else (least of all a parental figure) tells us to do.

Best that we share our own experience, give of ourselves---not advice---and offer our analytical skills. The rest is up to the listener.

Taking The First Step

S he sits on my office couch and speaks as if she is not even a participant in this drama, weeping and angry: "This divorce is his idea, not mine."

I understand her tears. Her marriage has fallen apart, and facing that reality is bleak. But this is our second mediation session, and she is resisting my efforts to get past this focus on her misery and focus on a plan for the future.

Reluctant to indulge her mood, I must swallow my impatience. I know she needs more time, so I continue to listen, and I hear:

"If only he would be reasonable . . . "

"Somehow I need to make him see . . ."

"I never wanted this, so it's up to him to . . ."

I want to tell her to stop howling at the moon but remain silent.

Her words are like those often spoken by people whose lives have been tipped off balance and are desperately seeking to regain equilibrium. They are actually a plea for change, but it is the other who is expected to alter their ways.

So, is it possible to shift, even reverse, another's point of view? Maybe so.

Her story illustrates the point:

This divorcing husband and wife were negotiating financial issues. He was adamant about paying support only in the amount his attorney told him a court would likely order, not a penny more. She insisted, and probably rightly, that he could well afford to provide a greater sum, which would allow her and the children to remain living in their current home.

On the other hand, awash in her own misery, the wife had made no effort to shield their teenagers from her conflict with her husband, and she had portrayed their father as the bad guy who was forcing them to move. Not surprisingly, it seriously eroded his relationship with the

children. He was hurt and incensed and blamed her for their alienation.

They were at an impasse, and at the end of our last session, both
walked off in a storm of irritation.

The next morning, when the wife called, she reverted to her now
familiar refrain: "If only he would be reasonable and provide enough
for us to stay here just for the next four years, the kids wouldn't resent
him so."

This time, wanting to keep her engaged, but moving forward, I
asked for her permission to offer some advice: "Sometimes when parties are deadlocked, if one person acts, unilaterally, takes even a small
positive step, it can cause an important shift in the relationship. Can
you think of something you might do to break this logjam?"

Her silence suggested she was finally ready and had heard me.

The next weekend, without requesting anything in return, she invited the husband to join her for dinner with the children, and in their
presence she apologized for having unwisely and thoughtlessly placed
them in the middle of their conflict. She explained that she and their
father were both struggling to create good outcomes. He relaxed his
stiff posture, and by the time dessert was served, tensions visibly
eased.

Will this magically bring about the hoped-for solution? Hard to
say. But the nature of their conversation will change in important
ways, of that I'm sure. Many bargaining chips remain on the table.
Talk will recommence. The impasse has been averted.

When a dialog has broken down, giving up on trying to persuade
another to change and taking a relatively small forward step, without
requiring anything in return, can generate a positive shift in the other's
perspective, allowing a new conversation to begin.

A Turnaround

Two days after he and his wife had attended their first mediation session, he phoned and said he was considering withdrawing, having come to believe that I was biased against him. I apologized and urged him to reconsider and keep the next appointment, reassuring him that I was determined to be neutral.

But I did not offer a denial. I knew he was right.

Inwardly, I excused my professional lapse. He had worn his arrogance like a badge. Self-righteous and proud, pointing out his many sacrifices, he had blamed the failure of his twenty-two-year marriage entirely on his ungrateful departing wife.

Covertly, I had cheered her on.

Arrogance, for reasons I do not fully understand, has always aroused in me a confusion of emotions: scorn, heightened anxiety, and perhaps even a tinge of fear. In my personal life I navigate the social scene to avoid significant involvement with those I deem to be narcissists.

But in my professional role, I could not ignore this man's perception of my bias. As a mediator, I had failed. Could I reestablish my impartiality and bring him back to the table to negotiate the terms of their agreement, and avoid his simply throwing down the gauntlet? Or would my inability to mask my reaction to his show of conceit and disdain send them off to combat?

I consulted a colleague who advised, "Try to genuinely empathize with how he's feeling, and if you can, let him know that you do. Unless you connect with him in this way, simply educating him about reasonable settlement options won't work."

Wondering if I could do so with sincerity, I determined to try.

At the beginning of our next session, I met with each party alone. In his early fifties, a vital, attractive and financially successful man, he exuded both assurance and despair. I deliberately put aside my previous mission of bringing him to recognize and accept the legal realities he faced. Instead, I simply asked, "Tell me how things are going."

He repeated the story of disappointment, innocence and blame that I had heard before, but now, having deliberately removed my attorney/mediator mantle, I listened as a friend might. I could genuinely empathize with what he was feeling: wronged, betrayed, misunderstood, and overwhelmingly sad. I did not, as I had before, try to get him to put aside these feelings. I actually felt a certain fondness for him. Sympathy requires only understanding, not affirmation.

This time my apology for my previous failure to fully appreciate his experience was sincere. I asked, "How can I be helpful to you?"

We talked at length.

He posed all the right questions. Working with someone who recognized and accepted his genuine angst, he could hear what I had to say. He was ready to be pragmatic.

I've learned something important. My earlier response to this man's arrogance had more to do with my past than the reality of his present.

We all develop ways to successfully perform our many roles as parent, spouse, and friend and in our work life. Over time what seems effective and comfortable becomes part of our standard script. Sometimes our assessments of the behaviors we witness are accurate. But at other times, without conscious thought or the wisdom of restraint, our reactions are responses to our own past experience, to emotional triggers that have little to do with the person before us. Then if our communication fails, we blame the other.

If our reflexive response to someone's words or actions derails a conversation, then we may need to question the source of our response. Listening instead with understanding and empathy, may cause a meaningful and positive shift in how we communicate and relate.

Which is how I hope to be received, when it is my crisis on center stage.

Mindful Questions

Whenever I talk with a close friend or a colleague, our conversation flows, unguarded. We are skilled players of the verbal interchange, asking questions, learning about the other, disclosing what is important about our lives or work at that moment. Ours is a dance with the steps so practiced, we have no need to be mindful about the questions we pose. We risk little, even with a misstep.

But that's not the case in other settings.

The cardinal rule taught in law school is "Never interrogate a courtroom witness without knowing in advance what the answer will be." Oh, the temptation is there to make one last probe to emphasize the essential winning point: *And why is that, Mrs. Jones?* Then a response that surprises us wipes out our earlier gains.

On the courtroom stage, the choreography of spoken words is critical, but need this be so in our personal or professional lives? Is the art of asking questions so important that it requires us to be mindful and deliberate?

Often it is. The way we pose a question can evoke a positive emotional response, an opening up, or just the opposite, a resentful apprehension. Here are some of my hard-learned lessons, which often I must relearn.

When negotiating, seeking to bring someone toward a desired destination and avoid a defensive response that may prevent or postpone agreement, the tone of voice of the inquiry, even the quality of eye contact needs to be free of all criticism or judgment. The distinctions can be subtle.

Ask: "Tell me about that." (open, accepting)

Not: "Do you really believe that?" (veiled belligerence)

Ask: "Would it be useful for me to explain my reasoning?" (respect, consultation)

Not: "Do you understand my point?" (intelligence called into question)

When a professional or intimate relationship is troubled, and discussion of an important issue has been too long avoided, either fearing a negative reaction which will only make things worse, or because embarrassment impedes honesty, before the question is asked, consider saying: "We need to have a difficult conversation."

Offering a person a moment to prepare, showing respect by not taking them unawares, may set the stage for them to willingly consider the concern at hand. If both conversation partners are off balance, just acknowledging this at the outset can avoid a defensive response, or closing a door.

And here's another rule it might be sound to consider: Some questions are best left unasked:

"Is this dress becoming?"

"Think I've put on weight?"

"Do you still love me?"

A Fable For Today

As a child, I was intrigued by *Aesop's Fables*, simple stories that ended with a moral. I didn't look for hidden meanings or seek to understand why the tortoise plodded on at such a steady pace to win the race. I just recognized that he had a tactic that worked. Here I present a fable, the tangled web of the player's motivation unexamined. But the message, the tactic that worked, is clear.

Paula and Jim were once intimate partners who revealed themselves to each other, perhaps one moment brave, another vulnerable and frightened. No pretense, no hiding.

But no more. Seated on opposite ends of my long office couch, both faced forward and avoided eye contact. Throughout the mediation session, their discussion seems almost dispassionate, their emotions well controlled. Except for occasional flares of veiled anger, their protective walls are invisible but real.

Paula hopes to return to school and work just part-time. To make this possible, she needs to move to a nearby state (less than two hours away) and rely on her extended family to help care for the children. Jim intends to remain in their former residence to provide the children a familiar home when they are with him. But paying the amount of support Paula requires to implement her plan could thwart his.

They're on a collision course. Paula says she's unwilling to accept any less financial support than she believes the court would order. Jim's clipped defensive response at the very mention of court is that the judge would never allow her to move with the children to another state. Each recognizes the power of the other's threat, but they continue to brandish their own.

Our session ended with nothing resolved.

From my earlier private meeting with each of them, I knew what they left unsaid when they were together. Paula, determined not to cry and appear weak in Jim's presence, had confided to me that to go from relying on someone she'd loved to relying on someone who had become a stranger and now loved another filled her with terror.

Jim, for his part, had confided his belief that by engaging in an intimate relationship outside his marriage, he had called into question his value as a father, even as a man, and surely as a provider. He was consumed with fear at the losses he faced.

The Court rulings that either of them might well achieve would frustrate them both.

Did what they left unsaid stand in the way of a successful negotiation? I couldn't be sure, but I knew that as matters now stood, reason would not prevail.

About a week before our next session, Jim called to inquire about some requested documents. I asked him if he knew how his wife was feeling. His response was immediate: "Sure, she's scared."

He added: "And frankly, I am too."

I suggested he consider giving voice to those feelings, letting Paula know.

Soon after our next meeting began, Jim turned and faced his wife. Although her eyes remained averted, he gently said, "I have some inkling of how scared you're feeling. I'm really worried too. I want us both to get a good new start, and I know having your family close will be reassuring and helpful. I've decided not to stand in the way of your move."

He acknowledged her insecurity and expressed his own. Her shoulders relaxed. A less tense, although tearful, conversation followed. Sadness and anxiety about the future did not dissipate, but now both parties were able to take tentative steps forward and compromise seemed possible.

The moral of the story: Anger is often driven by fear. Fears openly faced and shared may soften resistance to reason.

When Argument Is Futile

Although Dave and Jayne mutually decided they needed the intervention of a mediator, once they were seated in my office, they ignored me. Their conversation quickly became an argument, their voices strident. After a time I interrupted and asked, "Has this worked for you in the past? Do you manage to change each other's minds?"

They responded in unison: "Never!"

In recent months as their marriage crumbled, their lives had spiraled out of control, their teenage son a reluctant bystander. Now his grades were in free fall.

A friend had referred Jayne to a doctor, who diagnosed their son as having attention deficit disorder and prescribed medication. But Dave had grown up with an aversion to the use of drugs, particularly those that "fooled with the brain." He believed the problem was psychological, and he urged that all three of them enter family therapy or at least have their son work with a psychologist.

Jayne had no faith in Dave's approach---she derided talk therapy and "shrinks." She trusted the doctor who made the ADD diagnosis, and she spoke with other parents who described their child's miraculous turnaround on medication.

When I asked, both acknowledged that they were echoing beliefs held by the family in which they had grown up, although on this day they were armed with Internet research supporting their divergent views. Neither gave the other's data even cursory attention.

The question: Would either of them be able to give up their determination to change the mind of the other and agree on a plan to rescue their son? If not, would they have to let a judge decide? Both equally dreaded this path.

Although we may reject some of our parents' convictions, we do not often discard the viewpoints we adopted when we were young, in light of later life experience. We often discount as exceptional the evidence that doesn't fit with our basic assumptions.

Dave, Jayne, and I took a break for coffee, and when they were calm, they agreed to try a more pragmatic approach.

First we reviewed their present circumstances. Even if it meant restating the obvious, this placed them firmly in the here and now. I suggested:

*"You're both still hurt and angry, just beginning to heal."

*"Your son is struggling to keep his head above water in school."

*"So far, you can't agree on a plan, but you've each developed some possible strategies."

*"And you've decided not to turn the decision over to the Court."

Next we considered their choices and the possible consequences. The discussion that followed was less blaming and contained fewer references to the past. Eventually they developed these options:

*Dave agreed to meet with the doctor Jayne had chosen, if she would join him to talk with the psychologist he selected. She consented.

*Jayne suggested a joint meeting with their pediatrician, whom they had both always trusted in the past. Dave agreed.

*Jayne had already met with their son's teachers but offered to go again, with Dave.

We talked about where these steps could lead if both were committed to listen with an open mind. Either might change their view and proceed with the choice of the other, or not. But in any case, they would have more data, they would have heard it together, and been able to ask questions of the experts.

So a plan was in place.

The actual outcome: To avoid delay, Jayne decided to scrap all these appointments and start family counseling right away. Dave agreed that if after three months their son was still struggling with school, they would give medication a try. After family counseling began, they met with the doctor Jayne had seen and with their pediatrician.

Conclusion: Once partners set aside recrimination about the past and recognize the futility of argument, this process can work if they:

*clearly state the current circumstances that they must face;

*develop possible choices for moving forward; and

*analyze the likely consequences of each choice.

Sometimes, as with Dave and Jayne, just going through these steps can cause a shift from impasse to movement.

Caught Off Guard

I was knocked back on my heels. Not literally, but the impact was real, and my recovery was surprisingly slow.

The mediation sessions I was conducting with this couple had proceeded, at intervals, for several months. From the outset, the husband's intensity and his determination to control a situation in which he felt out of control, was clear. His wife was seeking a divorce he did not want.

On the first day of mediation, I always meet with each party privately. I ask about their negotiating style, aware of the importance of uncovering a history of past intimidation, whether physical or not.

At my session with the wife, she reported that at times during an argument he would shout at her and sometimes prevent her from leaving a room by blocking the doorway. But she assured me that after many months of counseling, she felt strong and believed she could withstand any undue pressure he might bring to bear in the decision-making process. I did not take this information lightly, but I proceeded anyway. Should I have known better?

As it turned out, she did well, but I did not.

After several months, they were almost finished, and only relatively minor issues remained to be settled. Pressing to quickly terminate the painful process, the husband made unrealistic demands she would not accept. Then, in my effort to lead them to compromise, something I said triggered a degree of rage I'd never before experienced. He shouted, not at her, but at me. Over and over he told me I was incompetent, that I didn't know what I was doing, and he loudly insisted they had wasted their time and money.

(In my later mental picture of the event, I'm seated, and he, a large-framed man, is standing and looming over me. On further reflection, I know that was actually not the case. When he rose, it was only to walk away.)

Did I fear a physical assault? I did not, even in hindsight, but his verbal blows hit their mark. My heartbeat was rapid, my breathing became shallow, and it remained so, off and on for days, as I repeatedly brought the scene back to mind.

I am well schooled in what to do on such occasions: Remain quiet, breathe deeply to calm myself, and take a mental time-out to refocus on my goal. Then try hard to understand what is going on in the mind of the one in the grip of negative emotion, try to calculate what has upset him to the point of verbal attack. I took none of these intelligent steps. In fact, I did just the opposite. When he raised his voice, I raised mine. I ordered him to leave. He would not. I countered his intemperate words with my own. The situation did not calm, but escalated. It went in waves, quiet for a moment and then crashing once again. Foolishly, I had failed to mentally prepare myself in advance, even knowing he was potentially volatile.

Roger Fisher, author and negotiation teacher from whom I've learned so much, asked a student in a workshop: "What are the three most important things to do in advance of starting to negotiate?" The right answer: "Prepare, prepare, and prepare."

We all negotiate every day, with a partner or spouse, a teenager, the dry cleaner. Most often we do so without much advance thought, and no immediate crisis arises, although over time tensions can build in our important relationships. Recently my local newspaper ran a front-page photo of a 14-year-old in a hooded sweatshirt, slumped on a park bench. She had run away from home after an argument with her mother. The number of runaways has sharply increased in recent years, the paper reported, and although most of these kids return home within a week, a third of those who do not end up selling sex to survive. After my own experience with this couple, I could imagine the argument that led to this serious breach, resulting in risk to the runaway child, and grief to the mother.

Might their encounter have gone differently had it been prepared for in advance? I plan to be prepared for the next time.

Slowing Down To Go Fast

They entered my office smiling, an amiable couple in their early fifties. After my introductory comments, they told me that even before deciding to mediate their divorce, they had pretty much worked things out. Many agreements were already in place, and they assured me they would make quick work of the issues that remained.

Approaching the end of our second session, Dave, a successful businessman, spoke with authority as he presented the financial plan he had devised for his wife, Kate, for when she would be on her own. Apparently listening, but quiet and no longer smiling, Kate did not react or respond.

I invited her comment. She just shrugged her shoulders. So I asked: "Do you need more data?" No answer, so I continued: "Perhaps you're feeling apprehensive about what the future holds?"

Still no response from Kate.

Leaning forward, Dave turned to me, making no effort to hide his irritation: "Wait a minute. You're putting words in her mouth. She's fine with this plan. We already talked it over."

At that, Kate came to life: "You don't know how I feel! I'll never find a job earning what you say I can earn." Now she was sobbing.

Dave sat back, displeased and exasperated. He thought the end was in sight.

So, why were they having this breakdown now?

All along I'd been aware that Kate was struggling to fully understand Dave's explanation of financial matters, all of which had previously been left completely up to him. He had pointed out that Kate had always paid the monthly bills, suggesting she was therefore savvy about finance. But did this follow? Although her husband treated her with respect and she did not appear distrustful, her anxiety was palpable. It's not an uncommon response when the reality of going forward alone is no longer inescapable. And Kate as yet had no job in sight.

Dave's impatience would not serve him well. That day, as Kate fully revealed her fears about the future, he came to realize that unless she felt more competent to engage and reason with him, and had employment she could count on, she would very likely turn to a surrogate power source--a lawyer, a gladiator--to do battle with her stronger opponent. That could make for a very long journey.

We took time out from mediation for Kate to meet with counsel wise in the ways of settlement, and a financial planner with special knowledge of divorce consequences. She took the time she needed to fully understand the deal she was about to negotiate, and she became assured she could successfully manage her financial future. She got the help she needed, but not from Dave. She began her job search and even researched the possibility of taking classes to enhance her employability. Taking these steps delayed the divorce by some months, but she was excited now, still wary but optimistic.

I've never been comfortable with the cynical comment that if both parties walk away from a negotiation equally unhappy, a good bargain has been struck. Rather, I think if both are given sufficient time to address their concerns, fully empowered, either alone or with a wise advocate at their side, they can reach a sound agreement.

I was confident that before long Kate would find her own voice. And Dave, even if reluctantly, came to realize that sometimes to go slow is to go fast.

No Woman or Man Is An Island

The case began when a mother petitioned the Court to terminate the plan she and her former husband had been following as they shared the task of raising their 8-year-old daughter. For years these parents had been working well together and their daughter was flourishing.

Then a disturbing event tipped the balance.

The father had remarried. His daughter and new wife gradually became acquainted and formed a comfortable bond. But, one evening there was a troubling exchange between his wife and daughter. He promptly phoned the girl's mother and asked her to come as soon as possible and get their daughter. In haste, the mother drove over and picked up the frightened youngster. On the trip home, she heard a tearful story: The stepmother had been drinking and when a glass of milk was spilled at dinner, she'd lashed out at the child, verbally but excessively.

The next morning the mother shared this story with members of her family. Her sister and her own mother strongly urged her to call her lawyer immediately and do whatever was necessary to prevent such an event from happening again. Days later she did just that. And soon afterward she filed a motion with the court seeking sole custody. Both parents were referred to mediation, and a week later they arrived at my office.

Now calmer and in a problem-solving mode, the mother knew well that even if she were awarded sole custody, her daughter's visits with her father, although fewer, would continue. The child's exposure to his new wife would not end. Father, in turn, offered evidence that both he and his wife took this lapse very seriously. She had re-entered a counseling program, had apologized to the child, and expressed sincere regret. In the weeks that followed, there had been no further incidents, and the youngster seemed relaxed, as eager as ever to spend time in her father's home.

When the mother and I talked privately, she recognized another reality: that her greatest assurance that her daughter would be protected in the future was her former husband's earlier decision to call her quickly and seek her help. Should there be another troubling event, he might not turn first to her again if she went forward with court action seeking to deprive him of his status as a joint custodian.

Our discussion in mediation continued and both parents explored additional ways to enhance their daughter's future well being. The father had already scheduled a family therapy session. He talked of how hurtful it would be to feel disenfranchised as a parent. The mother was understanding and seemed to recognize the damage likely to be done to their parenting relationship if she entered a public arena with allegations of fault and poor character. There was even tentative talk about the mother and stepmother taking steps to become better acquainted.

So did the mother drop the custody litigation? She did not. I urged her to return to mediation, but she refused.

The mother's family had maintained their pressure on her to proceed with the court action, even calling into question her devotion to her daughter if she did not. Her need to meet the expectations of her own family and keep their approval won out.

No one makes a decision in a vacuum. We seek the support and acceptance of our "constituency," our friends and family. Agreements need to be developed with this in mind, and in this instance I had not given that enough consideration. Although I was aware of her family's initial involvement in her decision to seek legal redress, I had not thought to help the mother develop strategies for sensitizing her family to the likely consequences of bitter and prolonged litigation. I might even have suggested that I meet with her family. Now everyone was poised for combat. The youngster was scheduled to talk with the judge in chambers.

It is so easy for extended family and friends to hold on to a winner/loser mentality without fully understanding the ramifications of parents undermining each other publicly, and in the eyes of their child. I chalk up this experience for future use. But it still feels like my failure.

Contemplate Winning

A confusing truth: When family issues are litigated, it is not always easy to distinguish a win from a loss.

For some time, a certain married pair have been unhappy together. Once they decide to end their marriage, the husband moves out of the family home, but he remains determined to have a significant role in the life of his six-year-old son.

The wife, angered by her husband's infidelity and rejection, repeatedly thwarts his efforts. Since their son's infancy, she had managed all of the day-to-day details of his life. She attended the school conferences and met with the pediatrician. Now she resists the father's wish to share the status of legal custodian and to spend significant time with the boy.

At one time, however, she, a registered nurse, was dependent on prescription drugs that she obtained illegally. He responds to her resistance by threatening to raise the issue of her addiction in court.

Both parties have ample ammunition ready at hand to publicly display their private misery, and some of their friends and family urge them on. Each meets with counsel reputed to be tough and relentless advocates. A custody contest is looming---when a counselor refers them to me.

In mediation, each party privately acknowledges that the other is a loving and responsible parent. And since his departure, the husband has proven that his new attentiveness to his son has staying power. The wife has completed a drug treatment program and, though still regularly monitored, has been reinstated in her hospital position. She is the one now being called upon to compromise, but she needs time and additional professional guidance to get beyond her bitterness and sense of having failed as a wife. It's not easy for her.

He needs to remain involved but slow down, ease up on the pressure and stay calm. That's not easy either.

Anxiety always runs high as an intimate relationship ends. *Will I be forever financially strapped?* the parties might wonder. *Will I ever find love again? Will I lose my precious connection with my child? Will another woman take my place with my son?* Preparing to do battle may temporarily quiet these voices. Fear sharpens the focus of both parties on all they stand to lose.

This is the perfect time to take a deep breath and a longer view. So I invite them both to switch gears, turn away from the pain of losing, and imagine winning the fight, either through threats and tough bargaining or by convincing a judge. Contemplate the aftermath of your triumph, I encouraged them.

These questions emerged:

*Will the losing parent back away from the parenting role?

*Will the losing parent tighten the purse strings, providing less generous support now and when college plans are made?

*Will parental alienation darken the life of one parent or the other, as they continue to denigrate each other?

*Will their son, forever caught in the middle of their conflict, be permanently damaged, his loyalty always questioned?

*Will their savings and future income be depleted by repeated litigation battles?

It's a sobering exercise, one that leaves more work to be done.

In the effort to regain control during the chaotic times of our lives, it is easy for us to become mired in misery, anticipating painful losses. Contemplating not just the fallout of losing a battle (or even a relatively minor argument) but the results of winning can actually restore some balance and lead to compromise and sometimes significant gains.

Look For The Longing

Divorced for a number of years now, they were seated on opposite ends of the long couch in my office. He spoke forcefully, complaining about some recent choices she'd made for their children. She listened with an air of detachment, occasionally meeting his angry gaze with a gentle smile, as if drawing a protective cloak about herself, immune to his verbal assault. Her calm presence denied, or at least refused to attend to, his emotional state. In the face of his fervor, she appeared to have the upper hand, but neither was winning.

Since their marriage ended, these intelligent and caring parents had worked reasonably well together. To all appearances, they were doing a fine job raising their children and loving them well. Their parenting styles differed, as did some of the values they sought to instill, but until recently they'd easily adjusted to each other's requests. But from time to time tensions built, and they sought help in the neutral space of my office.

On this day, they identified multiple issues for discussion and in doing so made obvious their mutual need for cooperation and accommodation. But the source of this father's current lament was not even on the list. He felt he was losing the close connection he'd had with their youngest daughter. She was entering adolescence and lately was making excuses to avoid spending time with him. As he spoke, his words gained momentum, and he became accusatory, blaming. His language escalated: *alienation, conspiracy*.

I tried to bring him back to their agenda and asked them both to propose some new options, suggesting they needed once again the give-and-take and understanding they'd offered each other in the past. He ignored me, too upset to pay heed. The session drew to a close, and he left angry and in haste.

I could not put him out of my mind. At some level, he must have known that his badgering manner and accusations would accomplish nothing. What was going on in his life, professionally or personally, that caused this train wreck of a conversation?

Did his anger serve to suppress his tears?

If I had a magic wand, I would decree that on his return to my office he would give voice to his worries without criticizing or blaming his ex-wife, which simply aroused her opposition. Under my spell he would request her help, and give sincere consideration to what she was seeking

And she would look for the longing behind his complaints.

Then, in an ideal world, they each would express appreciation for the many good things the other was doing for their children.

We will meet again. Lacking magical powers, I will offer them this advice but with humility, for I know that I have seen only the tip of the iceberg which is their relationship, and that much remains unknown to me.

But no matter how complex the dynamics of any alliance may be, to voice complaints without criticizing the other, and to look for the longing behind a complaint, are bound to further good outcomes.

Forget You

When my kids were very young, the ultimate putdown they could deliver to each other was "Forget you!"

This came to mind when I was rethinking a failed mediation with a high–conflict couple. One partner felt betrayed, the other misunderstood. In the tense conversation I witnessed, each frequently interrupted the other. They were denigrating and blaming. It was as if for each, the other's viewpoint had absolutely no legitimacy, their feelings no merit.

By the end of our meeting, I felt like a traffic cop, holding my hand up to silence first one and then the other, so a thought could be completed. Eventually they calmed, tired, and made an effort to comply with my no interruption rule. But by then they were dispirited and eager to leave.

As each in turn had taken control and silenced the other, the underlying message was: *You don't really matter.* Perhaps when an intimate partner has withdrawn their love, this is what we want to believe, but of course, they do matter, to each other and to their children, the current subject of their bitter discussion.

Had I accomplished anything with my no interruption mandate? Perhaps greater efficiency in addressing the issues before us. But would this intervention actually take them to a place of better understanding? Or agreement? Not likely.

What I needed to do was to somehow get them to stand in each other's shoes, to develop some empathy for what the other is feeling, and in turn, to be understood. If they were willing, this is the gift I would help them give to each other. The future benefits would be immeasurable. Even if only one of them were willing or able to take this step, it would result in an important shift in the nature of their negotiation. I am quite sure of that.

The ability to empathize and thereby offer respect to a departing partner (even if continuing to disagree with them), and a willingness to honor their past contributions to the family (often privately acknowledged to me), call for words that some conflicted partners seem unable to speak to each other. But, when they can do it, myriad conflicts evaporate, and it is wonderful to witness.

This couple did not return to mediation. I was sorry but not surprised. I'd planned to ask them to speak as if they'd exchanged identities, to tell the truth of the other as they knew it. Initially it would be awkward, but if they had been willing to persist, it would have been revealing, even exciting.

Could I have accomplished this without it seeming too contrived? Would they have resisted? Or might they have made the effort to imagine what their partner felt when repeatedly criticized for past deeds? And would they have asked if they were on target and really come to know the other's misery and not just their own?

Had they been able to do this, I think they would have moved forward. Will their children now simply inherit their pain and learn well the art of accusation and blame?

Pass The Salt

As our mediation session ended and Mark rose to leave, he turned to me and asked, "So, can we now tell our daughter what we've decided?"

I mirrored his smile. After a tense hour of talk, he and his wife, Ginny, had just made an agreement about how, once they separated, they would share time with their daughter. Recognizing the relief Mark felt, and his wish to cement the agreement, I said, "Sure, but remember you're telling her, not asking."

In years past, most mothers were full-time parents and fathers relatively uninvolved, but these two were fully engaged in their careers, and both played an active role in the life of their ten-year-old daughter. They were of one mind about the wisdom of ending their unhappy marriage, but each also feared that sharing time with their child might loosen a precious bond.

Mark had suggested that they simply ask their daughter to choose a plan. Ginny---wisely in my view---argued against it.

To many parents this approach---presenting the question to the child---seems sound, but some parents use it purposely to undermine the other parent, anger winning out over reason. When the child responds in their favor, they present it proudly, even quoting the specific language the child used.

The other parent cringes at the hurtful phrases attributed to their son or daughter. For example, "She says she'd be scared to stay with you and won't be able to get to sleep." Or, "He told me that he would much rather just stay at my house all the time."

When I hear such taunts, I quickly interject, "Best take those comments with a grain of salt."

But most parents ask for their child's preference with good intention. Then when the child seems to seek a special alliance with them, they are comforted. A neutral listener would readily recognize the child's need to please each parent, if indeed the quoted remark is even accurate. Very likely it is not.

During mediation with Mark and Ginny, I told them about research findings reported some years ago in *The Journal of Experimental Psychology*. The conclusion: Adults are likely to remember incorrectly whether information from a child was offered spontaneously or elicited through questions. And perhaps even more telling, adults are likely to confuse specific statements they made themselves with statements made by the child.

Dr. Maggie Bruck, a psychologist and McGill University professor, had twenty-four mothers with preschool children take part in a study in which the children spent twenty minutes playing in a room without their mothers present. Then the mothers were taped interviewing their children about their play.

Half the mothers had been told the research was focused on mother-child conversations. The other half were told they were participating in a memory experiment and should try to remember the conversation with their child as accurately as possible. Three days later all the mothers were tested.

Even the mothers who were warned ahead of time often incorrectly attributed statements they had made themselves to their children. And all were unaware of how many questions they had asked to elicit information. Repeated questions, even to an older child, suggest, and often evoke, a sought-after response.

I don't assume that divorcing parents who insist on the child's preference have malevolent motives. To some extent, we all hear from children what we want to hear. But healthy skepticism is particularly warranted about the reported words of children who are caught in the middle of parental conflict. Pass the salt.

CHAPTER TEN

SOLITUDE AND PRIVACY

Solitude

August approaches, the month in which Len died. Each year it is a time of looking back and summing up, a time that used to bring me low. It is less so with each passing year, as gratitude overtakes the sadness of loss.

How many of us ever seriously contemplate the likelihood that when we are older, we will spend years living alone?

May Sarton's *Journal of a Solitude* is a chronicle of her year of self-imposed isolation after an important relationship ended. She describes in great detail how she spent the days, her grieving and then her renewal. I loved that book and still remember the pleasure of vicariously sharing her daily experience. At the time, I was so engaged with my growing family and work life that I could only imagine such solitude. Now it is here, though not by choice.

Or is it?

When friends, or even family, invite me to join them for more than a few hours of socializing, I decline. Even if little else is on my calendar, and what is there could easily be put off, I will not willingly give up the time to myself.

I moved from my childhood home to a college dorm and on to marriage without missing a beat. Children, law school, the practice, life with Len. I rarely had moments that were not spent preparing for the next work or family activity.

So I did not give serious thought to this possibility of late-life solitude. The empty nest was never entirely empty. Even during my husband's last months, I didn't allow myself to imagine being without him. My life was the studied placement of one foot in front of the other. Goals were pursued, and my moments of reflection dealt with the present.

Now, for sixteen years, I've been living alone. It has been quite a remarkable, even a wonderful time of life. Are there anxious moments? Of course. Are there times of intense yearning for my past love? Yes. Occasional waves of grief still wash over me, but I now know they will recede in time, usually with the coming of daylight.

I surprise even myself with how much I treasure my solitude.

But then, I continue to engage with former colleagues, I often share meals with close friends, and I awaken many mornings to find a new email or text from a distant child. Without that, I might not treasure solitude. The human contact I have is a cherished part of my life and always will be.

I'm well aware of how my experience differs from those who are widowed or divorced in their middle years. Carrying on in the absence of a loved one, especially if they feel rejected, must be daunting, at least for a time. Then, I imagine, their need to start anew and build a different future fills their days.

Years of living alone lie ahead for many. Do they, as I did not, allow the thought to enter their consciousness? Will they too discover that those years afford an independence of spirit never before known, a life without pretense, authentic---a time to be savored?

Not everyone finds my destination, this peaceful place. A more troublesome past might harbor demons. I feel such gratitude for those who loved me so well that solitude is now a reward, rather than a sentence, offering time to occasionally look back and distill into words that which seems worth passing along.

Secrets Are For Telling

"Secrets are never kept. Everything eventually becomes known." These words, coming from an old friend, surprised me. I'd been describing the plight of a family I'm close to, in which secrets are eroding the relationship of mother, father, and adult daughter.

The couple were ending their unhappy marriage. They had told their adult children, and although disheartened, they were buoyed by the caring, respectful, even loving way their parents were making plans to keep the family well connected. While the parents were moving on to separate lives, they voiced no recrimination and placed no blame. Protective of their privacy, they simply told friends and family: "We've just grown apart."

Late one evening the husband wrote an e-mail to his wife detailing his distress about her infidelities over the years, which they had kept a secret just between themselves. His message contained no rancor, just disappointment and sadness, as he remembered things about their past that he continued to value.

She sent a reply e-mail, expressing remorse for having hurt him and told of her sadness.

Some days later their out-of-town daughter arrived for a visit. Before leaving the house to pick up some groceries, her mother asked her to access a neighbor's recipe sent by e-mail that morning. Opening her mother's computer, the daughter found not only the recipe but the e-mail messages her parents had exchanged days before. The secret was out. But later, rejoining her mother, she said nothing about the breach of her trust.

That evening she told her father about her discovery, and made known her anger and disillusionment with her mother. But fearing her mother's reaction, and adamant that her new knowledge not be divulged, she made him promise to keep her confidence.

Already in a delicate balance, the family now seemed poised for disaster. Privacy boundaries had been crossed, and their previously presumed open communication with each other shut down. A hidden bond between two family members excludes and distances others. And in order to maintain secrecy, the truth has to be distorted.

Did the husband, simply by writing the initial e-mail, display some intent to reveal the previously undisclosed reason for the divorce? When the wife sent the daughter to get the recipe on her computer, did she mean for her to find the e-mails about the adultery? My friend thought so, and to confirm his point said, "Secrets are for the telling."

I questioned that judgment, as we went on to talk about what had been concealed in our own families. I told him that I often wrote in a journal, especially when I'm troubled. Writing helps me sort things out. But what I write is private, I insisted, with no covert plan for disclosure.

"Oh, really?" he said. "And then do you destroy or save what you have written?"

I save it, but never consciously thinking about future discovery.

High profile male politicians most visibly prove the point when they leave a letter to a new soul mate where a wife can find it, pay for furtive sex by check or with a traceable bank transfer, or meet for an assignation with the press hard on their heels. Do they believe themselves to be invincible, or are they inviting exposure?

We keep some secrets in the sincere belief that others will be hurt more than ourselves in the telling, to the benefit of no one. But by turning a truth into a secret, is it always a truth we wish could be known? Is it only if we are known fully, and our secrets accepted and forgiven, that we feel loved for who we really are, or were?

Do we hide, all the while wishing we could pop-out like a jack-in-the-box and be greeted with approval, no longer keeping the lid on?

So if the music box is wound, the music plays and the catch is released. Well, accidents happen. Right?

The Little Notebook

Sometime after my husband's death, I emptied his desk and found a small spiral notebook jammed into the very back of the top drawer, apparently long forgotten. Written on the first page was a date in April, five years earlier, followed by the name of the neurologist who had diagnosed Len as having Parkinson's disease, a day sharply etched in my memory.

We had both noticed a slight drag of one of his feet, but just weeks before he had fallen when snowshoeing in the Cascades with our son-in-law and turned an ankle, so it was easy for me to discount his awkward gait. What I did not know at the time was that Len had become aware of a significant change in his handwriting, the letters becoming small and cramped.

This symptom was one key to the initially suspected, and later confirmed, diagnosis. That morning we left the medical office building and sat in the car wrapped in each other's arms, but only for a moment. There were no tears. Len calmly drove us home. He was meeting this news as he had past challenges, with a stoic determination to just keep moving forward.

In this newly discovered little notebook of his, beneath the name of the doctor, Len had written:

Make changes:

*live by the water

*wilderness fishing

*more joyous times

I stopped reading after those three final words, and for a moment I was uncertain about turning the page. But in mere seconds I made my decision. Without further exploration, I tossed the notebook into the large trash bag at my feet, which already held the detritus of the other drawers.

Over our years together, unless offered, we never read each other's mail. Rarely did we even share phone conversations with our kids. Sporadically, I wrote personal reflections in a journal, but I didn't hide it away. Without ever speaking of it, we honored each other's privacy.

But after his death, was his privacy still a consideration? Was that really the cause of my decision, or was my refusal to continue reading born of something else entirely? Might "more joyous times" imply a hidden dissatisfaction with his life, with our marriage?

Len, a man of few casually spoken words, expressed himself in writing clearly and with insight. Both of us would, from time to time, put on paper what was troubling us and later share what we'd written or the concerns crystallized in this way. Eventually, we talked and talked. Sometimes wept. Always, we came together. That was no longer possible.

Looking back, I believe this was my thinking as I briefly held the small notebook in my hand: Five years had passed since he'd written those words. Whatever secret yearnings they described on first learning of his diagnosis might later have become part of our conversations, may even have led to some meaningful shifts in our lives. There were many. But then again, perhaps he'd decided not to reveal to me the private thoughts he'd had in mind on that fateful day.

We owe no one complete disclosure. Control over the sharing of thoughts and feelings, the choices we make in the daily dance of caring for a relationship, is ours alone.

Privacy is eroding in the public arena, in ways both seen and unseen, but it can remain as protected as ever in our personal lives. When we share a confidence with a trusted friend, or even when a friend asks us, in words or wordlessly, to keep a thought to ourselves, we can still relax with the knowledge that our privacy is assured.

As I tossed the little notebook aside, I knew, with barely time to take a breath, that the memory of Len I wanted and cherished was the memory of how he chose to be known to me.

The Unobserved Life

Are young people today first stirred to shared sexual arousal in cars? Decades ago, in the years before co-ed dorms, even before the pill, we were able to slide across the bench-like front seat, whether moving or parked, and snuggle close. No bucket seats or cup holding consoles to form a barrier.

But, this brief essay is not about sex. It's about private space, the unobserved life that cars offered then, and in some ways may still do.

In 2007 shock-jock Don Imus made front-page news with his mean spirited verbal assault on the Rutgers women's basketball team. I had never been part of the Imus audience, but the episode was widely reported and opened a window on this brand of controversial and often offensive talk radio. Many expressed surprise on learning that hundreds of thousands of listeners made these commentators a lucrative source of advertising income for the broadcasting networks and earned these uninhibited boy-men millions.

My query: Why are these shock-jock radio personalities so popular?

Attempts have been made to analyze the audience of those angry white (mostly) men who celebrate insult. Although sexual innuendo is pervasive, they don't provide eroticism as Lenny Bruce did in the 1950s or *Hustler*-type displays of blatant sexuality. Instead they target specific groups for denigration: women, blacks, gays and now Muslims.

At the time of the Imus rant, I was reading Richard Ford's novel, *The Lay of the Land*. His everyman protagonist, Frank Bascombe, is a realtor. Driving in the New Jersey countryside, either alone, or with colleagues or clients, he conducts business but also has many meaningful personal conversations (often with himself).

"Why do so many things happen in cars?" Bascombe wondered, "Are they the only interior life left?"

Time was when men in workplaces could share sports talk or gossip at the office water cooler, or ogle nude pinups in the back room. These impromptu gatherings afforded an opportunity to exchange the latest sexist or racist joke or slur. No doubt for some this was innocent fun, but for others it was a way to assert their power and status as superior to those being ridiculed

This workplace behavior went more or less unchallenged until the 1980s, when women employed outside the home achieved a critical mass. They called into question behaviors that had hitherto been acceptable. With the backing of supportive men, receptive legislators and concurring jurists, they expanded the definition of sex discrimination in the work setting and the word *harassment* entered our common vocabulary. The term *politically correct* was also born and bespoke a new standard, received with delight by some and with a cynical sneer by others. In any case, the rules began to change.

One analysis I found persuasive suggests that many of those resenting society's new rules tuned into drive-time radio and listened to mocking racist and sexist put-downs, happily unrestrained and free to guffaw or gloat. For except in their cars radio was most often a shared (observed) family experience.

Radio shock-jocks are now a dying breed, although some of these shows have moved online. No FCC restraints. And as workplaces become more diverse, personal relationships are formed and those previously deemed the "other" become known, better understood and respected. Many embrace the new ethos. But private spaces still abound for those drawn to vulgar jokes and aggressive talk. They only need a Twitter account or to put on a headset and download a podcast to be once again secure in their unobserved lives, not ready to cast off a way of thinking still so deeply engrained in our culture.

To me it seems a sad and lonely pastime, nowhere near the pleasure of snuggling in the front seat of a car.

Does Love Trump Privacy?

When our youngest child grew up and moved away, I claimed her bedroom and fashioned a space all my own. It was quite small, on the second story of our home with leafy tree branches almost touching the windows, a nest of sorts. Sometimes my husband came and stood at the threshold to ask me a question, but he didn't walk in. He never entered uninvited. It was our unspoken understanding, as natural as breathing, that our separateness was respected. This personal background sets the stage for my describing a mediation session in which a privacy issue arose.

The couple working with me made it clear they were not seeking therapy---which was fine because it is not my skill. Rather, they wanted to preserve their marriage by negotiating a specific concern: The week before, without consulting his wife, the husband had installed a lock on his home-office door. She was hurt and angry.

His side of the story: Recently while he had been away from home, his wife had opened a piece of mail addressed only to him. Reading it, she learned that his business debt was considerably greater than he had let her know. On discovering this, still in his absence, she looked through his desk and files, and eventually explored the content of his computer. Upon his return, she confronted him. He was outraged. That was when the lock went on.

Her side: She firmly believed there should be no secrets between marriage partners and that she was therefore perfectly justified in her actions. He was the one who had much to explain.

The response I addressed to her was spoken without hesitation, or sufficient forethought. With some fervor I said, "But everyone is entitled to a zone of privacy."

My statement and my tone surprised them, and myself as well. With hindsight I regret the unprofessional manner in which I spoke. I should have posed some neutral questions to each of them, not been judgmental. Predictably, the issue did not get resolved in my office. Later, when the wife called to cancel their next scheduled appointment, I learned that after further discussion between them, her husband had removed the lock from his office door.

Another client discovered that her husband had read the journal in which she wrote each morning on waking. She was incensed, even though she'd kept it tucked in her nightstand drawer, readily accessible. "How could he not understand that it was for my eyes only?" she asked me.

Will such unwelcome intrusions as these continue to rankle over time? My guess is that insistence on full disclosure, even on knowing their partner's innermost thoughts, is more likely to erode harmony than to foster it. Are these wounded loved ones likely to become more secretive or less?

Why is privacy so important? The very notion of "invading" our privacy suggests a significant violation, an assault on our autonomy, a piercing of that protective skin we seek to keep intact (so many words of aggression!) Privacy keeps us safe, free of judgment until we are ready for exposure, and then only to those we trust.

The Introvert's Dilemma

Picture this David Sipress cartoon: Two coup les meet on a street corner. One of the men has placed his hands over his eyes. His female companion says, *"It's too late, Roger . . . they've seen us."*

For decades I yielded to the social plans of those friends more gregarious than I am, but I developed a practice of making furtive early departures from group events. Over time it evolved into my Rule of Two. I rarely visit out-of-town friends or family for more than two days. And if I'm part of a convivial gathering for more than two hours, it's only because I haven't found an acceptable way to escape.

I did enjoy the spirited get-togethers of my high school years, but even then, after the first couple of hours, I was content to become an observer, never the lasting life of the party.

In college, pairing off began in earnest, for me a lovely respite from collective fun seeking. Marriage followed and soon thereafter came graduate school for Len, when we had little time for the festive company of friends, no money, and babies to care for. Home became a safe haven from the social whirl.

Was I anti-social, as some suggested? I thought not, but then why the discomfort?

Then one day a friend wise in the teachings of Carl Jung tagged me as an introvert. *Surely not* was my immediate thought, for I love working with people and treasure many friendships. But with this idea in mind, I began to read about the distinctions between extroverts and introverts, and soon gratefully accepted the label.

Author and journalist Jonathan Rauch, an introvert himself, wrote about this personality dichotomy for *The Atlantic* (an article that for years drew more traffic to the magazine's website than any other). He affirmed that we introverts need hours alone every day. We love quiet conversations with intimates about how we are feeling and what we are thinking. But when we cannot avoid attending social gatherings of more than three or four others, we need days to recuperate. We are not shy, as may sometimes be assumed, and we can even be comfortable making formal presentations to large groups. We are not anti-social, not depressed. But when the jovial schmoozing starts, we yearn to sneak away unobtrusively.

Rauch writes: "For introverts, to be alone with our thoughts is as restorative as sleeping, as nourishing as eating."

Extroverts are energized by being in the presence of others, whereas introverts are the opposite. Brain scan research suggests that the two groups process information differently. So this is the root of my Rule of Two. I need no longer feel deficient or make excuses. I can walk into a room feeling no obligation to be who I am not. I allow myself to be a listener, am comfortable (usually) alone within the crowd, then leave.

Friends and the disappointed marriage partners who were my clients often asked, "Are introverts better off partnering with extroverts or with someone of their own orientation?" I have no simple answer, but I'm sure that if opposite types are to be happy together, they need to recognize and accept each other's bent.

At some point Len and I voiced our shared reality that dinner parties were a dreaded chore rather than an anticipated good time. For the first two hours, it would be fine, but then our furtive sidelong glances would convey a mutual yearning to go home and have the rest of the evening to ourselves.

We were both introverts. I do wish I'd better understood this early on. I would have worried less during his retreats into silence. But over the years, as we came to know each other so well, many times we were comfortable alone even when together.

For those of us who are introverts, an unplanned meeting or a mandatory social gathering finds us bemoaning the fact that *It's too late, Roger, they've seen us.*

No Need to Explain

"How can I explain this to my folks?" my young friend asked. Two months earlier her husband disclosed his infidelity, and she had found shelter and solace with her parents. Now after that separation, she'd decided to return to her own home. Since leaving, she and her husband had gained important insights in counseling sessions, both together and on their own, and they were ready and determined to repair their relationship.

But in comments both subtle and direct, her parents cast doubt upon her decision. They pressed her to disclose her reasons for changing direction. Their anger toward their son-in-law was great, and although at the outset their daughter found their attitude comforting and supportive, she now regretted having shared such a private matter.

My immediate response to the question she posed was: "You don't owe anyone an explanation."

Countless times I've said this to friends and clients. But her startled reaction gave me pause. Was I just playing out some old rebellious script of my own? My tendency when I was younger, and someone made an overture or stated an opinion that I wanted to reject, was to try to legitimize my decision by articulating a well-reasoned rationale. Even declining a dinner invitation seemed to call for an extended explanation---never just a simple: "Sorry, I can't make it."

Looking back, I think I failed to note an important distinction between just giving voice to my choices, stating what I believed to be the best path to take, and the need to justify my choice, to meet some norm of social acceptability. Often I'd hedge, be less than forthright, resenting what I accepted as an obligation to comply with the standards or expectations of others, while at the same time resisting the invasion of my private thoughts. I'd end up feeling somehow the one at fault.

No longer. That view has long since been discarded. Stating a personal preference or decision need not be followed by an effort to legitimize the choice. Responding to a request for a full explanation may or may not make good sense, depending on who is asking. It is important to share underlying motivations or personal reasons with an intimate partner or an adolescent child. Such a conversation deepens understanding, which is always of value.

For a while, it seemed at least once every year the infidelity of some prominent political figure or celebrity was exposed, often followed by staged contrition on network TV. If the wife stood mutely by his side, she would be derided by many and judged unkindly. A microphone would be thrust before her and she would be asked for a statement in response. I cheered those who declined and decided to maintain their privacy and offer no comment, or simply to absent themselves and avoid the public eye.

A few observers, who might identify themselves as feminists, scorned these women for remaining steadfast in the damaged relationship. From my perspective, no one has the right to invade the privacy of or pass judgment on another's intimate relationship.

As for my friend, whose parents insisted that she provide reasons for her decision to rejoin her husband in the weeks that followed, she resolved her quandary. The essence of her considered response was: "I appreciate your concern. I've given it a lot of thought and in my judgment, it's the right thing to do. Whatever problems we have will be ours to solve together."

Their questions persisted, but she did not waver.

Seeking to explain one's own or another's actions, invites appraisal by those whose standards or values may well differ from our own. That is something we can be open to, or not. Our choice, not someone else's due.

CHAPTER ELEVEN

MOVING ON

Valued Only In The Marketplace?

At the age of 84, Justice Ruth Bader Ginsburg rejected retirement (and so did I). For a number of reasons, many postpone taking this significant step: diminished savings following an economic down turn, the desire for the continued enjoyment and challenge of the work at hand, and our extended life expectancy. Most of my retired friends appear to be happy with the decision, finding it to be a time of new beginnings, with freedom to pursue postponed passions. But some descend into a depressed mood. So I wonder, does retirement have hidden or unspoken aspects that one may not realize until the office door is actually closed? A story comes to mind:

Since I left the house where I lived for more than forty years, I've moved four times, each time to less space, jettisoning many belongings. Len and I were least willing to part with the art we had collected over more than five decades, and those works with greatest meaning still surround me and lift my spirits.

One such canvas is by an artist of some note who lives and paints in the Northeast. In the 1960s, when my mother was aspiring to become an artist, she studied with him, and a close friendship developed. I greatly admired his beautifully executed impressionist oils that hung in my parents' home. Some had a haunted quality--understandably, as they derived from the suffering and losses of the artist's family during the Holocaust.

As the years went by, his work was exhibited in well-established New York galleries and sold for ever more substantial sums. I kept up with his advancing career when I talked of the art world with my mother. Then in the mid-1980s, she visited with his family, he then sixty-seven, and learned that his paintings were no longer being offered for sale.

This is what she told me: At the height of his career, the artist was diagnosed with a serious illness and was given a guarded prognosis. In response to this news, he made a pact---with whom I'm not sure---that if his illness was arrested and his health restored, he would never again sell another painting. Was this simply magical thinking, challenging death? Perhaps, but not entirely, for even before this ominous health forecast, he had begun to question the negative impact of commerce on his own work and that of others. Free of "the market," he thought, he could explore wherever his art (or muse) might lead.

Subsequently I learned that his health was restored. He continued to paint, his work ever more evolved, but it was never again sold. The family lived on savings and on his and his wife's incomes as teachers.

Some years after my mother died, my husband and I were traveling through upstate New York and decided to make a detour and visit the artist's home. We were greeted warmly and soon shown into a climate controlled storage facility in the basement. It was overflowing with what appeared to be well over a hundred canvasses, the collection of more than two decades. It was a remarkable feast for our eyes but seen only by those who traveled to his modest country home. And they still were not for sale.

As we talked, we learned that in the years following his pledge to no longer sell his work, he had offered to donate paintings to museums and universities that had previously been eager to obtain them. Early on a few accepted, but thereafter most did not. Puzzling. Apparently, because his work was no longer being exhibited in galleries and sold at exalted prices, their value was called into question.

Query: Does one's labor, one's past achievements, or even one's very identity lose status unless it is currently assigned monetary value? At least in this case, it apparently did.

And what of my colleagues disappointed in retirement? Do they feel they are no longer valued if they cease to be professional problem solvers active in the marketplace? Looking back, their status may be secure, but looking forward? Is this part of what motivates some of us who find it so hard to close the office door?

And then, of course, are we slowing down the hands of time?

The Anniversary

Should I write about this? Uninvited, unwelcome images intrude as I lose my hold on purposeful thought.

The anniversary of Len's death is near.

Sixteen years ago, as summer was ending, the man who was my love, my companion for more than fifty years, left me. Sometimes that is exactly how it feels. And each year as August approaches, I tell myself: *Not this time, gloom will not have a place at my table.* Surely I am wise enough and strong enough not to succumb to these unbidden thoughts anymore.

During that last year, even as his health steadily declined, we shared an incomparable intimacy. Caring for the body I knew and loved so well. Touching him, being touched by him, pretending we had many years to go. Sadness and joy so entwined.

Our marriage was perfect. Our marriage was imperfect. We had exquisite times of closeness. We had brooding times of silence. We always shared respect and caring. We were bound, but free.

At the end of that August, as soon as my family departed, I returned to my world of work. At home I welcomed solitude, and relaxed times with close friends, long postponed, began again.

I busied myself with the tasks that attend such a loss. I sent out notifications. I closed accounts. I sorted, disposed of, or gifted books, papers, and clothing. To one son went the music collection, to another the tools, to a grandson the fishing rods and lures. I kept for myself the treasured letters and a few favorite warm shirts.

Then, as the first anniversary of his death approached, my steps slowed, my throat tightened, and my quiet times became more somber.

Disbelieving, I silently wailed, *Why should this foreboding of the calendar cast me down?* But it did, and it has each August since. *Can it be that I'm not the wise and strong person I insist I am, unable to rise above this annual malaise?*

I consult with a counselor, who says, "The very angle of the sun, as the same date approaches, casts shadows reminiscent of the days you choose to forget. The leafiness of the trees, the heat, the hour of first morning light, all of these images appear unbidden and take you back to the heartbeat of that time."

This I can understand and accept. And I can share with others whose intimate losses are known to me. For them too, anniversaries presage low times.

Now I tell them that each year I mark the anniversary in a significant way. I do not let it pass unnoticed, as once I hoped it would. Instead, I picnic with friends in the park where we used to go to as a young family. I revisit art galleries that we wandered together. I share a special dinner with an intimate. I go to breakfast at the home of dear friends with some old pictures in hand.

Len and I seldom gave each other gifts, although we often urged the other to buy something yearned for, something that we would not purchase without a push. A painting. An airplane!

So every year, as the day approaches, I buy myself an anniversary gift, a thing of beauty: A small sculpture of a horse's head. A Murano glass sphere. Beautiful Italian soup bowls. A tiny Netsuke cat. An iPad.

This year it is a new home, which I am molding to please my aesthetic eye.

He would have insisted.

Insulted?

As the baby boomer generation approaches what used to be the assumed retirement age of sixty-five, media sources and social networks report that they anticipate extending their work life. Some seem eager to continue work they enjoy, and others wish to build retirement portfolios, while still others have hit their stride in their fulfilling careers. Until recently, I was with them, and frankly happy to have their company, not to feel like such an outlier.

But the thought brings back to mind what happened to me on a windy day almost ten years ago.

Walking home from my office, I met two young lawyers with whom I have a passing acquaintance. We paused on a busy downtown corner waiting for the traffic light to change. They were empty-handed and carefree, dressed in sweats. I carried a briefcase, my heavy winter coat open to the warming spring air.

We smiled in greeting and one of them said, in a jocular tone, "Bea, you still working?"

I answered "Yes."

Then the other said, "Come on---it's about time you packed it in and got out on the golf course."

The light changed. Side by side we crossed the street. At the far corner, they walked on, while I turned toward home, saved from having to respond. In the days that followed, I chewed on their words as a dog might worry a bone.

Every friend I chanced to talk to heard about this insult. But why did I think it was an insult at all?

After much thought and conversation, I came to see their remark as friendly needling. But I had taken it as an irritant. Why? Was it because I was already sensitive about my age? Did I hear in the message that I'm expected to retire, to move over, if not to play golf, then at least to get out of the way? I think so.

My husband joyfully retired at sixty-three, after thirty years of college teaching. Disillusioned with a university administration that valued successful research grant applications over skilled teaching, he contentedly entered a new phase of life and spent the next fifteen years engaged with family, our household, and trips to wilderness fishing spots he could reach in his small plane. I happily continued practicing law.

Both Len and I were raised by parents who became parents as stock markets crashed and the Great Depression followed. Len's father yearned to retire to escape from the crushing physical hardship of his blue-collar life. He longed to fill his life with music, travel, and raising beautiful flowers. My father, also having risen from poor beginnings, joyfully gave up the competitive business world to enjoy leisure, listen to music, and read.

Neither of our mothers ever really retired, Len's mother helped care for each new grandchild she could hold close, and mine, an artist, was still painting just weeks before her death at eighty-nine.

Dare I generalize from this small sample?

Perhaps when in control of the work we've chosen to do, answerable neither to productivity demands nor to the discordant values of a system we no longer feel able to influence, we can cheerfully soldier on, fulfilled by bringing to bear competence learned over a lifetime.

And after all, aren't the eighties the new seventies?

Difficult Moments

On a Sunday afternoon, I walked three city blocks through a gentle rain to spend a few hours in a favorite place, the public library. Planning to just browse for a while, I was surprised to hear music coming from the large atrium performance space. Before a seated audience, sat (and stood) a jazz trio. The piano player interrupted the flow from time to time to explain the interplay of the instruments, the improvisation. I wandered in and settled behind those already gathered.

My fellow listeners were young and old, some in families. A few children played at their parents' feet, paging through books. Colorful rain gear completed this inviting scene with its mix of downtown residents and visitors. That the music had drawn us all together filled me with pleasure.

An older couple was seated just in front of me. The man casually put his arm about his wife's shoulder and pulled her closer. They exchanged brief comments and smiles now and then, during lulls in the music.

As the minutes passed, my throat tensed and tears filled my eyes.

In the years since the death of my husband, solitude has often been my companion---a welcome, comfortable companion. But here, quite unexpectedly, I felt painfully alone and found myself overwhelmed with sorrow. In the midst of the closeness of others, partners and families in a setting not unlike one I'd shared so often with Len, I imagined how much he would have enjoyed this experience and yearned for his touch. My sadness eclipsed my pleasure.

I left, catching my breath and collecting myself on the walk home. Remembering it, even now, the tightness in my throat returns.

Here's what I wonder: When I'm alone, I often warm myself by choosing to recall happy memories of my dear lost love, feeling lucky to have shared so much of my life with him, and to have matured together. I sometimes reread letters we wrote so many years ago and those are satisfying. A contradiction? Out in public, with others about me, I must accept his absence as the painful reality. I cannot pretend, not even for a moment.

I understood my sadness in the midst of such an enjoyable experience, and also my need to leave. Do people who have suffered painful losses draw into themselves, some even isolate themselves, to avoid reliving even happy events which make the loss so much more present?

The Memory Lapse

Is there anyone over the age of fifty who doesn't experience a fleeting moment of worry when they can't remember the name of a familiar person come upon in an unfamiliar place, or the title of the book they were reading just the night before?

My former law partner and I meet weekly for lunch. As we walk about town, we are often approached by someone we both know we know. Our forward steps slow, hoping one of us will be able to come up with the first name, for then the other can almost always retrieve the last. Together we have an entire intact memory. We joke about our lapses, but a trace of unease lingers.

Last week my unease grew.

On Thursday I spent time with a friend about six years my senior. We'd been neighbors many years ago. She and her husband now live in a retirement community, and we meet only occasionally. After we get caught up with the lives of our children, our conversation usually reaches into the past.

On this day it seemed as if every other person either of us recalled, or his or her spouse, had a dementia story to be told. I drove home under a cloud of dread.

A few days later I traveled with two companions into the Indiana countryside for a Labor Day visit with friends. Sitting around the dining table, we discussed the difficult decisions our host was facing about the care of her eighty-nine-year-old mother whose memory was fading. I welcomed the intimate and meaningful talk. Silently I felt reassured, recalling the mental acuity of my mother at eighty-nine, until I brought to mind my father's emerging confusion at the age of eighty-two.

Later that day someone asked me about books I'd recently read. I couldn't remember the title of the one at my bedside, although could describe it as a memoir. Again unease.

Perspective returned the next day at the office, as I performed competently, attended to projects, reviewed and shortened task lists. But did the dread linger somewhere in the recesses of my consciousness? Yes.

As the day was ending, two colleagues walked into my office to talk about a planned new venture. We were all tired and happy to relax in each other's company. As is my habit whenever I need to dispel worry or want reassurance, I told my story. I described my lunch meeting with the old friend and also told them of my Labor Day memory lapse.

My associates, considerably younger than I, smiled and nodded. Then one commiserated by saying he frequently reads a particularly interesting op-ed article in *The New York Times*, and an hour or so later recommends it to his wife.

She will say, "Oh, really? What's it about?"

He will respond, "Well, just read me the first paragraph and then I'll tell you."

What a wonderful friend to give me this temporary reprieve. I walked home smiling.

A Melancholy Day

When my kids were young, Halloween was my favorite holiday. At little cost in time or money, the night ended with costumes askew and each child's candy hoard spread out and sorted on the living room floor. Apples were disdained, while chocolate was eaten with abandon.

It seems right that Thanksgiving should be next in line for favored holiday status. It is a time to remember all that we most treasure, friendships and family, and to savor favorite recipes. It seems right, but is no longer quite true for me.

When this day arrives, I join with loved ones, and we all smile as a sumptuous meal is presented. But I have to purposefully hold myself back from talking too much about who is no longer at the table. Perhaps I will talk about him casually, even tell a funny story about his turkey carving exploits, and then I will be able to breathe again. But after a time I will want to go home, be alone with my thoughts, and allow my practiced smile to dim.

Last Thanksgiving, as the day waned, my older son phoned from another city and sensed my mood, one he said he shared. We reminisced about years long past, our annual early Thanksgiving morning drive to the Chicago suburbs, for the gathering of the Larsen clan. The kids, snug under blankets, dozed in the back seat, then awoke as dawn lightened the sky. On reaching the halfway mark, we would pull into a familiar roadside restaurant for pancakes and hot coffee.

When we reached our destination, the small prairie town where some Larsens still live, the aromas of the feast filled the air. Cousins fairly tumbled over each other in joyful reunion. We were too many to all sit together except around the Ping Pong table in Aunt Joan's basement, so hot dishes were carefully carried down the dimly lit steep cellar stairway. Babies were passed from arms to arms, giving new parents respite.

How many times did this scene replay? Then one day our children returned to their childhood home carrying their own small people aloft on shoulders grown broad and strong. The familiar aromas were then in my own kitchen, which was soon crowded with helping hands. As the day drew to a close, Len and I would leave for an evening walk, hand in hand in the cold winter air.

Soon another Thanksgiving will have passed. Everywhere I'll hear: "How was your Thanksgiving?"

The response: "Great!"

My response: "Fine."

In this answer there is both truth and undisclosed sadness, not just my own. For every family, the holiday evokes stories of remembered pleasures and joys, some sadness, some regret.

Oddly, I almost savor my melancholy mood, for it intensifies the moments I remember. Would the losses be so mourned if they were less precious?

But if I were king of the world, once Thanksgiving brings on our thoughts and words of gratitude, we would fast forward to the first of January, bypassing all the holiday merriment of December. How humbug is that?

Moving On

Some years ago several close friends, in or nearing retirement, found the perfect place to live: a cluster of five small condominiums nestled at the base of a wooded park, close to downtown, yet secluded. They phoned and suggested I consider living there as well, as another unit just across the courtyard was now for sale.

Just at that moment, a long hiatus from work over a holiday period had left me with a heightened sense of what post-retirement loneliness might feel like.

I was moved by their invitation, for it came along with a tender offer of the help I might need as I grow older. If my car wouldn't start, or if my human apparatus begins to fail, friends would be close at hand. I warmed to the prospect of this new shelter, both the roof and their arms.

I went to look around. Their new home was in the very neighborhood Len and I lived in for more than forty years. The park, situated at the top of the hill and visible from their windows, was the place we had walked together several evenings each week. Our children had rolled head over heels down the steep slopes on new spring grass and sledded on snowy winter evenings. So this would mean a return to loved surroundings.

But as I peered through dark windows into this promise of a new haven, a cloak of sadness enveloped me, and I knew this was a move I never could make. I abandoned the idea in the blink of an eye.

Needing to explain my change of heart, both to my friends and to myself, on my return home I listed the pros and cons. There were many, but one alone outweighed and made the rest irrelevant.

While I was visiting the house in the park, memories of my former life with Len arose at every turn of my head, his absence a constant presence. He had never set foot in the cozy downtown loft where I now lived. Many times a day, I glanced at his photos, even had imaginary conversations from time to time. But I brought him in at will---he came only by invitation. Then his presence, not his absence, was the essence of my mood. I had some control.

Each of us chooses to make the past a part of the present in different ways, accommodating to our unique circumstances and needs. I felt strengthened by this experience, able to recognize and then act on my feelings, to manage my life looking forward, determined to create my future security in new ways, even if I would be more alone.

But just one year later everything changed. A friend, a retired colleague, called with a fearful message: "I've fallen and can't get up. Will you come and let the Life Squad in?"

Within the year I moved to that new haven close to the well-remembered park.

A Thoughtless Greeting

It used to be when they reached the age of forty, then fifty, now maybe even fifty-five, that women notice that no one is noticing. Add an additional ten years for men. Most of us make peace with advancing invisibility as we age. We can take pride in what we've become, what we've learned, what we are still able to achieve. Then, surprisingly, even a small stab can deflate a well-earned sense of self.

Here's my story.

I am visiting a new doctor, a well-reputed specialist. The waiting room is crowded, many of the patients past middle age, some very elderly with another in attendance. The office staff exudes efficiency and a friendly ease.

Before long I am ushered into a small examination room, one in a row of six or seven.

An assistant administers eye drops and asks some basic questions, noting my answers for the busy physician to review when he arrives. She smiles, offers a magazine, promises a not too long wait, and leaves me alone.

Soon I become aware the doctor is in the examining room next to mine. He is talking to someone about reapplying for a driver's license that has lapsed, the tests to be anticipated, and how to avoid likely obstacles. The patient must be hard of hearing as the doctor's voice is raised. His tone is gentle, unhurried and indulgent. The listener's responses are barely audible.

I find this doctor's caring way heartwarming, and appreciate the sensitivity with which he addresses the elderly patient who I assume is vulnerable and confused. I will praise this kind doctor soon, when we meet.

He knocks and enters, smiling, and with his hand outstretched in greeting says: "Hello, young lady, how are you doing?"

I feel diminished, categorized, even disrespected. I am not young. Please, doctor, do not call me "young lady." It strips me of dignity. Young women are 35 and under. You can use my full name, or no name at all.

But these words, although screamed, are unspoken. I simply say *hello*.

I swallow my rehearsed words of praise for him.

I have lived many years and value the richness of my experience. I've had joy and sadness, both in good measure, and good health, all of which allows me to look to the future with optimism, accepting, if somewhat grudgingly, the deficits of aging. But I want my status to be recognized, not made into foolishness.

Did the doctor view his manner of greeting me as a kindness, or was it simply thoughtless ineptitude? And does it matter in the larger scheme of things?

Yes, it does.

Going Home Again

I have a decision to make: should I revisit the past, or stay away from the scene of love now lost?

I've been invited to join some former neighbors at a progressive potluck supper, moving from house to house on the street where Len and I lived for over forty years and raised our family. After leaving seventeen years ago, we returned a few times for holiday picnics, but now if I go, I go alone.

It turns out that the first house on the schedule is our old home. A wave of sadness washes over me when I imagine walking up the porch steps and over the threshold.

I ask friends if they think I should go. Hearing the catch in my voice as I pose my question, friends urge me not to. Aware of my sorrow, they talk of their own past losses, empathizing with my reluctance to give up the distance I've already gained. But as they probe and express their concern, my thoughts become clearer, and my need to overcome this foreboding actually strengthens.

The beauty of these conversations, even if tearful, is that they meet the feelings head-on, whereas ever since the invitation arrived, and they surfaced, I put them away unexamined and decided not to go. Now I wonder. Perhaps I can go and be rewarded in some important way. Perhaps I can face my unease rather than be its victim or later have to live with regret.

My old front door opens, and I am standing in the entryway. I am enveloped in the memory of the many reunions held in that very spot, when I welcomed Len's return from a geologic or fishing trip. In such sweet moments, a sensual embrace renewed so much love.

The changes made by the new owner of our house don't keep me from visualizing the favored chair in which Len so often sat reading or listening to music, gazing into the near distance, lost in private thoughts that might or might not later be shared. I spent many early morning times in that same chair, preparing for a challenging work day ahead or, having wakened in the pre-dawn hours, thinking through and pushing aside a cloud of unhappiness.

I approach the wall that held the old upright piano where our three-year-old son stood and picked out tunes with perfect pitch, the first signal of his future as a gifted musician.

The kitchen sink, beneath the window with the view of the ravine-like back yard, yields the memory of the giant rope swing that evoked Tarzan-like yelps from my kids and drew neighborhood children in droves.

I walk out to the sun porch where my eighty-nine-year-old mother spent her last few weeks cared for so tenderly by Len, who was by then retired.

As I stand there, I also remember hard times, hours of loneliness, worry, or discord, experienced most often as silence rather than spoken aloud, only later to become food for thought and reconciliation. That too was part of the fabric of our family.

Sooner or later grief sweeps into all our lives. For now, revisiting old memories, securely embraced by friendships of the present, trumps the pain of loss and even enriches past joys.

Invisibility

The publishing world is shrinking, so friends ask why I still talk of writing a book. Striving to be truthful, I answer, "To avoid becoming invisible."

They object, especially those who are younger, not wanting me to feel diminished by growing old. They would like to talk me out of having this concern. But they cannot, for I'm a realist, and know that aging eventually brings a retreat from center stage.

One particularly close friend pursued the point, "Do you mean invisible as a woman or in a more general sense?" she asked.

"Both," I said.

As women grow older, we accept a measure of invisibility. As we advance beyond the ever-expanding stretch designated midlife, it threatens us in earnest. As we walk down a sidewalk, male heads no longer turn, no eye contact is sought. But with family and friends, and professionally, we can continue as vibrant, seasoned, and more accomplished players years after feminine allure has faded. It's not a bad trade-off.

Only a Pollyanna would insist that nothing has changed when the step slows and maintaining bone and muscle is an ever-greater challenge. We spend many hours developing future plans with the knowledge that even the wisest plan may go awry.

For me, writing now keeps the stage lights on. And recalling memorable experiences, both personal and work related, exploring and crystallizing their meaning and crafting a story, offers a new role, a revival, a second act. Is this a universal dream for those growing older, to pass along what life has taught them? Is it a dream for the not yet so old?

To those dear friends who seek to reassure me of my continuing relevance, I've apparently failed to communicate that becoming less visible is not all bad. So here's the good news for me, which will eventually be true for them:

I'm no longer burdened by ambition. Though eager to enhance my ability as a writer, I have no more mountains to climb.

The skills I developed over many years of professional practice allowed me to serve the needs of clients caught up in distressing times with calm assurance. Younger colleagues often seek my advice, and their expressions of gratitude warm my heart.

A new generation is coming forward to assume leadership of volunteer projects that remain important to me, permitting me to enjoy the role of valued advisor and engaged spectator, leaving me precious hours for my own design.

Never again will I wear uncomfortable shoes.

The clothes in my closet are classics, by my own definition. Being in tune with fashion matters not at all.

Without guilt, I no longer attend social events I think will be tiresome.

Responsible only for my own timetable, I can talk with a friend for hours, even in the middle of the day, should we both choose.

I'm no longer a consumer of anything other than consumables. Well, that's not entirely true as I am part of the Apple world. But simplicity allows me to have greater focus and enough time to become technologically savvy.

I don't have to pretend, so as to be perceived in a favorable light. I don't have to hide who I really am. Invisibility has morphed into transparency.

I'm less visible perhaps, but I'm not marginalized---only centered.

Borrowed Clothes

I delight in my Sunday morning ritual: I forego the usual weekday exercise routine and return to bed with coffee and *The New York Times*. But last week, as I hefted the paper onto my lap, I felt the fabric at the elbow of my pajamas gently give away. It wasn't because this iconic newspaper was so weighty, but because my sleepwear used to belong to my husband, Len, I alternate between wearing the light blue and the maroon.

I have a clear memory of buying them. We were together at a department store. Although he was still robust in many ways, Len's over-all health was in steady decline. His legs were no longer taking commands from his Parkinson's-compromised brain, and he rode in a wheel chair. Our eyes were wide open to the fate we silently anticipated, but somehow purchasing new clothing was a way of challenging it. Instead of speaking the words, we sustained each other by touch and we embraced normalcy, pretending there was no end in sight. Why not?

Within weeks of Len's death, I packed up almost all his clothing and took the collection to Goodwill, keeping only some favorite shirts, the pajamas, and a down filled winter coat.

Although the coat swallows me up, it envelops me with warmth and delights me as no woman's coat ever has because of its myriad hidden and external pockets in which life's essentials can be carried. The zippers on the coat have not yet failed,

A number of the shirts I've kept have leather elbow patches that I attached, and on some the cuffs have begun to fray.

And now the pajamas, worn nightly, may be on their way out too. I will not give them up easily, for all of this borrowed clothing has made me something of a cross dresser, as I cloak myself with fond memories of the intimacies we shared.

Why is it women can wear men's clothing without comment or scorn, no raised eyebrows, while men donning women's clothing would immediately raise questions about their sexual identity?

In my long ago high school days, it was the fashion for girls to wear outsized men's sport coats paired with pleated plaid skirts, bobby socks and saddle shoes. And in 1950s romantic movies, risqué or adventurous females wandered yawning and barefoot from the gentleman's bedroom attired in his shirt and apparently little else.

During World War II, as men marched away, women replaced them in important roles on the home front. Rosie the riveter wore slacks to work--- teenage girls put on the power clothes of men a full two decades before Betty Friedan picked up her pen and launched the second wave of the woman's movement. But as the war ended, women had little choice but to relinquish those roles.

Later, when women began to enter the market place in large numbers, they traded shapely frills for the cover of severely tailored suits, staking a visible claim to the authority and power previously ceded to men. Was that a step up? And do men take a step down when they soften their appearance in any way?

Having "arrived", the feminine figure is again on display, in the boardroom, and the courtroom, occasionally even with a hint of décolletage.

But for me, wearing these borrowed clothes is quite simple. I'm not making a political statement, just enjoying sweet moments remembering Len's presence.

Off Balance

In the years since Len died, I've become a reluctant traveler. I find reasons to put off planning a journey, even when I anticipate pleasure at my destination.

This is not a response to 9/11 or to long security lines---I've always been comfortable on commercial flights. And I've long been accustomed to traveling alone, as Len and I often visited our distant children separately, knowing we were able to connect with them more intimately this way.

So what's going on?

As I've made a determined effort to think through this self imposed limitation (at least what's available to me on a conscious level) and get beyond it, the source of my aversion is becoming more clear. It is humbling to realize, and then acknowledge, that what is standing in my way is embarrassment.

For years I've adhered to a personal rule never to visit anyone for more than two days, so I always travel light. But lifting even a small rolling suitcase into the overhead compartment, at best awkward, has become a challenge. Then I arrive at an unfamiliar or ever changing airport, get temporarily lost in a crowded maze, and am not absolutely sure which ground transport to use to get to my final destination. All of these difficulties give me pause.

Of course, it makes no sense. There are always kind people more than ready to give assistance, and I know that well. But somehow when I'm on my own, I need to feel and appear completely competent and in full control.

In some way, this new reticence may relate to the loss of my partner. To Len, I could disclose any vulnerability or failing. In the telling, I would suffer no embarrassment at all, and I would receive comfort and reassurance. Confiding in him, or even just knowing I could later phone to report some misadventure, my travel troubles lost significance.

So recently I've begun to disclose these weaknesses to my children and close friends. Doing so has generated interesting conversations about the unique sources of embarrassment for others, sources quite unlike my own but equally limiting, and some of significant import.

This emotional state, embarrassment, is not shame for some hidden moral wrong but simply a witnessed loss of dignity. For others as well as myself, the need to avoid drawing unwanted attention to some perceived personal flaw objectively makes no sense but induces us to hide these "defects" from public view---and even influences our decisions.

An important truth I recently read sparked my decision to put these thoughts into words: *Embarrassment is the death of possibility.*

And here's another: *To take a step forward, you have to momentarily lose your balance.*

The Pleasure of Touch

My cat likes to have her ears pulled. Her eyes narrow, and she arches her neck with pleasure as she awaits the next gentle tug. This feline resists being picked up, but curls into the crook of my arm when I am propped up in bed reading. She nudges, seeking my touch, and the pressure of her warm purring body is a sweet reminder of the relaxed heft of a sleeping baby.

Some months after Len died, one of my younger friends took on the role of the caring daughter and gave me an unusual gift: a massage by a therapist she admired. When I told her this was something I'd never done before, she said, "Everyone needs to be touched, and you're alone now."

I went, and continue to go every now and then, welcoming this time of complete ease and pleasure. The therapist always begins by massaging my feet, and though I only spoke this thought aloud after many months, whenever her skilled fingers knead these muscles, I wish I had done this for Len, especially in his last six months when he was in bed more hours than usual. For this man whose feet were almost always on the go, it would have been a special way to express the sweetness of old love.

It is easier to write of my cat and a masseuse than of the sensual pleasures of my marriage, but there is a point in doing so. For us, the promise of touch was ever present. The gentle pressure of my fingers on the back of his neck as he drove, his hands easing my tensed shoulders as I sat at my desk, holding hands in the movies or nestled together when watching TV---intimate touching renewed our appetite for life.

Now that I'm alone, though engaged with others during the day, my patterns and pleasures have changed. I enjoy my solitude, but it differs from a past shared with another. Evenings, I no longer watch programs or movies that I suspect will cause me to feel anxious. When we watched the news together, leaning into each other, no matter how fraught the coverage, I was safe, moored. Now I check the Internet for newsworthy events the next morning, in the light of day.

On Sundays I often reread Len's old letters. His words and his handwriting almost feel like a touch, a lingering memory of the pleasures we shared, which can quite take my breath away. Then I close that door and reenter the present with a sigh but no anguish, knowing I can return.

Comfort with touch is tied to family history. Mine was a family in which physical affection was open and easy. Len's family was just the opposite---casual touching was rare, foreign, even uncomfortable. When he and I were first together, seeking physical closeness, I consistently walked him off the sidewalk onto the grassy verge. It was a lasting joke between us that spoke volumes. I eventually converted him.

Lest this become a maudlin description of an idealized marriage, I also well remember the hours, sometimes days, when we didn't touch, lay back-to-back and distant in bed, or silently left the house for a solitary walk. But being deprived of touch inevitably brought us to talking, so much was it the glue of our marriage.

So why write of this? The importance of touch is well established. Infants need it to thrive, and now studies are proving the same is true for adults. Breaching the chasm of being alone in one's skin, and experiencing or giving pleasure, can lower blood pressure, reduce stress hormones, and improve immune function.

So, a reminder for those with the good fortune to have a loving partner at their fingertips: Massage their feet.

A PERSONAL HISTORY

Both of my parents emigrated from Russia, my mother as a toddler in 1900, my father at sixteen, in 1907. Along with other family members, they were escaping the violent pogroms designed to eliminate Russia's entire Jewish population. They came on ships that docked at Ellis Island, and they soon moved into the homes of family members who had preceded them and settled on the Lower East Side of New York City.

On arrival, my father, Joseph Rosenblum, speaking no English, enrolled in high school. After graduation, working days and studying nights, he attended New York University, eventually completing law school. He was conscripted into the Army when the United States entered World War I. In 1918, he returned to civilian life, but not to the practice of law. Anti-Semitism was then an acceptable norm in professional ranks, so law firm employment was out of his reach. Without a financial stake to practice on his own, he entered the world of business where his legal education served him well.

My mother, Sadie Skoletsky, five years younger, left high school at sixteen to work as a pattern designer in the garment district to support her widowed mother. She married my father in her early twenties, and over a period of just three years, she took only brief interludes for the birth of her three children. Birth control education and devices were then illegal, but my mother, determined to live life on her own terms, found her way to the hidden offices of the birth control pioneers who bravely risked arrest. For many years, she worked side by side with her husband. Then when she was forty-seven, and I, her youngest child, left home for college, she left the world of business to pursue her new goal: To become an artist. Over a number of years she sought out painters of note whom she admired and convinced them to accept her as a student. In time she was recognized as an artist of note in her own right.

In significant ways, Len's family background differed from mine.

His mother's ancestors arrived in Maryland in 1650 as indentured servants. His mother, Leora Bowen was born in Eagle Grove, Iowa, at the turn of the last century, the seventh of eight children. When she was just five years old, her mother died of tuberculosis and by the time she was ten, her ailing father could no longer care for her or any of his children. After a short stay in the Iowa Children's Home, Leora became a ward of the state and was indentured to a family that owned a bakery where she worked and cared for the younger children until she was eighteen. During her only year in high school she met her future husband who also left high school to work after just one year. They were both eighteen when they married. She bore four children and became the matriarch of the family, nurturing and strongly influencing both her own family and the families of her grown daughters, offering to step in whenever troubles arose. She never identified herself as a feminist, but although gentle in demeanor, she was strong and determined as she played out the family centered care-giving role expected of her generation of women.

Len's dad, Merrill, was born in South Dakota, the third of living children. Four other siblings died young. His father, Lars Larsen, had emigrated from Norway, and the family spoke Norwegian at home. Merrill did not get along with his father and ran away when he was sixteen, lied about his age, and joined the National Guard. Initially stationed on the Mexican border, he was sent overseas just months before World War I ended. Unschooled, he was brilliant and creative, an accomplished self-taught pianist who did not read music. For most of the years I knew him, he worked as an electrician for the railroad, even outside in the bitter cold of Chicago winters, until his death.

Organized religion did not play an important role in either of our childhood homes. Both of my parents were raised in the Orthodox Jewish tradition, but by the time they married in 1921, they had cast aside the religious beliefs of their families, drawn to the rationalist secular teachings of the social reformer, Felix Adler, who founded the Ethical Culture Society in New York in 1876. Ethical Culture was a movement, sometimes designated a religion, established to promote greater justice in human relations, without the trappings of ritual or creed. It was with these values that my parents raised their children.

Len's family attended the Lutheran Church only sporadically with little emphasis placed on religious teachings. Len's dad became a Freemason. The Masonic Lodge became a regular and important meeting place with fellow thinkers.

Not only were our family histories far different, we also grew up in opposite political worlds. Just months after my birth, the infamous stock market crash of 1929 presaged the Great Depression that over the next few years brought the country to its knees. Suited business-men stood on street corners selling apples, while others jumped to their death from high-rise buildings, becoming iconic symbols of eco-nomic despair. In one of my early childhood memories, at about the age of three, I am standing at the edge of the driveway of our home. It was in foreclosure, and we were awaiting the arrival of the moving van. I was blissfully unaware of my family's economic peril.

Four years later, on March 4th, 1933, Franklin D. Roosevelt was in-augurated as U.S. President, launching the New Deal era. Liberal leg-islation---Social Security, public works programs, the National Labor Relations Act---all became part of the new political landscape. Forev-er after, FDR was the hero of my family lore. As I grew up, his wife, Eleanor, was even more significant. She travelled the world, wrote a daily newspaper column, became a United Nations luminary, and most importantly for me, received my father's open admiration. Many years later, I came to realize that his praise for her in my early years gave me permission to be assertive as a woman, even though I was born into a time that fostered the image of the ideal woman as an ever-supportive, smiling helpmate, deferential to her decision-making hus-band.

If FDR was a hero in my home, in the rural Illinois home of Len's youth, he was the consummate villain. Although politics were not frequently discussed in Len's home, at that time his family and friends were conservative to the bone.

The day after the December 7th, 1941 attack on Pearl Harbor, the United States officially entered World War II, already raging in Europe for several years. In 1943, at the age of nineteen, Len enlisted in the Navy. He left behind his exclusively Caucasian and Protestant community and entered a new world, coming to know men from many walks of life and religious and ethnic backgrounds. Training in electronics and sonar revealed his aptitude for science, and he was selected to teach these skills to recruits.

After the war, soldiers returned to civilian life, and college campuses were flooded with veterans seeking to make up for lost time. In 1944, passage of the GI Bill provided servicemen and women with financial support for higher education, including a stipend for basic living expenses. Not widely known, or simply ignored by us at the time, this celebrated post-war period of renewal and economic growth also perpetuated rampant racial discrimination. African American veterans struggled to receive these benefits. Most did not. Frequently the recipients of this largess were the first in their family to have the opportunity for full time study beyond high school. One of these was my husband-to-be, Len, who in 1946, after three years in the navy was college bound.

Meanwhile that fall, at the age of seventeen, I left my home in suburban New York City, also headed for college. The long train ride into the Midwest remains memorable, as it was the first time I'd ventured away from the urban East Coast where I had tested early adulthood in the exciting metropolis of New York City, where the unusual was commonplace, and diversity, both of thought and the land of one's origin, was celebrated. Books and movies, my only reference points for more rural or smaller urban communities, presented them as having a sameness, a homogeneity. I accepted the conventional wisdom that Midwesterners followed the rules, that they stayed on the curb until the walk light flashed, instead of dashing across a busy street, dodging approaching cars.

Fate brought us both to Antioch College in Yellow Springs, Ohio.

There we met and fell in love, held hands in public, and enjoyed intimate cuddling whenever a private space could be found. A year later, still chaste, we traveled to the small prairie town of Villa Park, Illinois, forty miles west of Chicago where Len's parents and his nine-year- old brother, Curt, lived in a home they rented from an elderly woman who stayed on as a sort of esteemed border. They greeted me warmly, this stranger from New York City. Only years later did I learn that after our visit Len's mother asked him if I was Jewish. He responded wondering if that mattered. "Yes" was the answer in her next letter. But their discomfort was apparently fleeting, for there was never a moment in all the years that followed our first meeting, that I had cause to feel unwelcome or unworthy of their loving ways. Initially, my father also questioned the wisdom of this mixed marriage plan, as my mother told me only after he died. Both of my parents loved Len and treated him like a son. Prejudices were eroded by familiarity.

In 1949, while we were both still students, we married under a large oak tree in the backyard of Len's geology professor, joined by a small number of family and friends. I had just turned twenty and Len was twenty-five.

Upon graduation in 1951, we were off to New York City, Len to attend graduate school at Columbia University, and I, newly pregnant, to establish our home and fulfill my expected and accepted role as wife, homemaker and soon-to-be mother. Five years later, with a new PhD in hand, Len began his teaching career as an assistant professor of geology at the University of Cincinnati. By the end of the decade, two young sons, Neil and Grey, and a baby daughter, Julia, completed our family. Like most women of my postwar generation, I assumed without question that at least until our children reached adulthood, the role of wife and mother would be the design of my life with Len the breadwinner. Ours was later designated the "silent generation," known for its focus on family and career over activism. But as the 1960s approached, that was all about to change.

In 1963, our youngest child, Julia, was four years old and attending a morning preschool program. Homemaking chores without a little one underfoot no longer seemed meaningful. For the first time in years, I had time on my hands and started to wonder: what next?

How often do unplanned incidents, unexpected turns of fate, cause a shift in direction that profoundly changes a life's trajectory? Perhaps more often than is realized. Three events caused me to take an exciting new course.

In the spring of 1964, a neighborhood friend brought me a copy of Betty Friedan's *The Feminine Mystique*. Published the year before, it was a catalyst for the second wave of the women's movement. (Only in recent years did I learn from the daughter of this generous friend that this gift from her father was his way of removing it from their home before his wife picked it up and read it.) I read it eagerly, identifying with the stories Friedan told as each chapter unfolded.

In the summer of the same year, Len joined a group of academic geologists for a six-week course in Scandinavia leaving the kids and me to develop our own summer adventures. The four of us piled into our 1957 Chevy station wagon and drove first to Columbia, Missouri, to visit good friends. At dinner on our first evening in their home, the husband, a professor of economics at the University of Missouri, asked me what I planned to do next, a question that likely would not have been posed just five years earlier. My vague uncertain response led him to comment on my interest in social issues and then, without fanfare, he suggested that I go to law school.

I was startled. The idea came as a total surprise, but as the kids and I drove on to northern Illinois to visit with Len's family, the thought was rarely out of my mind. Days later we drove halfway across the country to New York's LaGuardia airport for a joyous reunion with Len on his return to the United States.

My memory of the drive to Cincinnati the next morning remains vivid: Len is at the wheel of the car, the windows are open to the breeze, and the kids are engaged with books and crayons in the back seat. Unsure of what response to expect, I tentatively pose the possibility of my attending law school. Without a pause, he responds, "What a great idea. Perfect for you!" In retrospect, how differently my life might have unfolded had his response been critical or dismissive.

My path to the legal profession began in the fall of 1965 when I entered law school, and our two-career life began. Three nights a week, I left the house as Len returned from his workday to take over the feeding, bathing and bedtime routines of our children. As I had previously fostered his career, he was now ready to champion my new life, taking on a nurturing role that otherwise he would not have experienced. Often he later proclaimed, "The women's movement was the best thing that ever happened to men."

In 1969, I was one of only two women in my graduating class of 44 newly minted lawyers, and at the age of forty, I began to practice law. The only women in law firms at that time were secretaries and paralegals, but the Legal Aid Society was welcoming and that was where my legal career began.

For eight years, I fulfilled my Perry Mason dreams as a public defender, ultimately serving as the director of the office with a staff of twenty-four attorneys, most of whom were young new law school graduates who were passionate about fighting for justice for the underserved.

In 1980, I opened my solo law office with no idea what issues I would be asked to address.

As a public defender, I had been called upon to be in court virtually every day, prepared to be in litigation mode. So by the time I entered private practice, my trial skills were well honed. Coincidently, in the mid-1970s, the divorce rate had begun to soar, so many clients whose marriages were ending walked through my office door. I stood ready to take up their cause. The adversarial system was my touch-stone.

But after only a few months representing parties in the Domestic Relations Court, I realized that while my good trial skills often result-ed in "winning" the case, my client's delight was short-lived. Every win carried with it too many losses. Even with my measured ap-proach, courtroom confrontation, and the public exposure of intimate private disputes, generated so much hurt and bitterness that parties struggled thereafter to treat each other with civility and respect. Funds put aside for college educations were depleted to pay legal fees. Months, sometimes years, of litigation left families in shambles. Chil-dren, faced with increased family turmoil, were too often drawn into taking sides, caught in a loyalty trap, and permanently damaged. Trial outcomes were unpredictable, as judges often imposed their own mor-al worldview on the cases before them. Not infrequently the parties who'd lost felt they'd been wronged by the judicial decision, returned to court, and filed a new motion, determined this time to be the win-ner.

I did not want to remain part of this destructive process, but for a time there seemed to be no other way. I concentrated on developing my negotiation skills, believing I could enhance my ability to work with opposing counsel to settle the case and avoid courtroom animosi-ty. This proved useful, but required like-minded opposing counsel. Sadly, I too often encountered lawyers who equated zealous represen-tation of their clients with doing battle, giving little thought to the af-termath.

In the mid-1980s, in the effort to hone my negotiation skills, I spent time over four summers at week-long intensive workshops stud-ying at the Project on Negotiation at Harvard University. There I first learned about the field of mediation and soon realized it was the an-swer I was seeking.

In 1987, I served as the first woman President of the Cincinnati Bar Association. Some years earlier, my friend, attorney Robert Rack, had established the first mediation office for the U.S. Sixth Circuit Court of Appeals; now we developed a plan to establish the non-profit Center for Resolution of Disputes. I chaired the board of trustees and when the Center opened its doors in 1988, a new mediation mission was underway.

My contribution to the family income helped with our children's college expenses and allowed Len's wanderlust to flower. He purchased a small plane, and began to fulfill his lifelong dream of exploring every region of the country, often with geology students, and searching for the perfect wilderness fishing spot. He even flew off with the two other women in his life, his mother and our daughter, then fourteen, on a flying adventure to Alaska.

A different way of life began after our daughter left home for college. We were free to reclaim an even greater measure of independent choices. All three of our grown children moved to distant cities as their own families and professional lives evolved, so travel for visits and holiday vacations with them provided years of family adventure. As we passed beyond our middle years, Len's illnesses began to intrude, hastening his retirement from college teaching. But his continuing determination to fulfill his longing for adventure was undeterred. Even in the final months of his life, when he was confined to a wheelchair, his friends carried him off for a weekend of ice fishing on a northern lake.

For me these were heady years of professional achievement that blended with evenings and weekends facing Len's mortality and finally experiencing the sweet intimacy of caregiving until the very end. Len's death at the age of seventy-eight, in 2002, brought our fifty-three year marriage to a close. An unlikely pair at the outset, we grew up together in a union that encompassed many different marriages.

In the years that followed, I welcomed solitude at home each evening and a vibrant professional life with each new morning. I went on to mediate well over a thousand family law matters until late 2017, when at the age of eighty-eight, I closed my office door.

Looking back, I review and write about the insights we gained over the years, as we became ever more known to each other. Times of companionable closeness were interspersed with silent, albeit respectful, withdrawal. Most often we were happy and comfortable in each other's presence. Although we fared far better than the troubled partners I worked with professionally, we were never soul mates, that ideal state of being all things for each other. As our intimacy and understanding of each other grew, so too did our recognition that we could allow each other the freedom to pursue different dreams. For me, my intensity about my legal career that drew me to the office six long days each week. For Len, the opening of the eyes of his students to both an academic and on-the-scene knowledge of the earth's formation and beauty, and after retirement, the freedom to fly off into the wilderness to hike or fish with like-minded companions whenever the time and the weather was right.

Overall we lived joyously within our union but also as quite separate individuals on our own paths. From the very beginning we shared a belief system and basic human values, perhaps essential keys to a lasting loving connection.

ACKNOWLEDGEMENTS

Expressing gratitude should be easy, but it is not. The rewards I've received along the path to this book becoming a reality, from colleagues, friends and professional allies, are difficult to reduce to a few sentences. Yet, that is the task.

Some history: Although I've been writing essays, either for print or radio broadcast since 1994, the concept of publishing a book first came to mind in 2006. My radio commentaries ended in 2002 when the station was sold. A few years later my mediator colleagues and I moved out of the building in which we had worked together at the Center for Resolution of Disputes for the past eighteen years. I was seventy-seven years old and retirement appeared imminent. My oldest son, Neil, an academic and published author, suggested I write about my professional and life experience and taught me how to create a blog, and for some time I regularly posted essays in anticipation of one day publishing a book. But life took a different turn, and retirement did not happen for another twelve years. Although I continued to offer commentaries online and wrote articles for the Cincinnati Bar Association Report, the book would have to wait.

My husband, Len, found his way not only into my heart but also in later years into many of my essays. We met at Antioch College in the 1940s, married while still students and grew up together, supported each others' careers and dreams and grew old together, offering us a time of incomparable intimacy in Len's final years. I continue to be thankful to him for his love and respect, and the courage he always displayed in the face of adversity. Daily, I call upon his example.

From my three dear children, Neil, Grey and Julia, and my son-in-law Howard Levine and daughter-in law Cindy Kallet, I have received the gift of steadfast kindness and compassion. Cindy even provided wise editorial counsel as the early structure of the book was taking shape.

It was my friend, attorney Ken Germain, who in recent years provided the nudge to reconsider a book, a compilation of a body of work. He has been relentless, an email here, a lunch appointment there, with the persistent question: "How's the book coming?" Ken also drew the interest of his colleague, Steve Gillen, who generously offered his time and expertise in exploring publishing options for an attorney audience through the American Bar Association. This was not the right fit and the project languished.

Fast forward to 2016, when editorial consultant Howard Wells offered his services and encouragement as book editor, having read a number of my online essays. When I demurred, he asked the essential question, "Why are you writing your essays?" It was not hard to answer this question---"to share with others what I've learned over the years." He forced me to confront the inconsistency of that motive and my reluctance to seek a wider audience. Raised in an era when girls were taught to wait to be chosen, saying the words, "I am writing a book" was breaking the rules. This mature, well-received professional woman hung back and needed a push. Howard provided it and has offered his wisdom ever since.

It was my great good fortune to reconnect with Janet Biehl after many years. The daughter of one of my lifelong dear friends, Janet, a noted author herself of numerous social ecology works and a highly sought after freelance book copyeditor, agreed to work on my manuscript. Her skillful repairs and suggestions and her enthusiasm for my writing gave me permission to accept the lofty designation: author.

As the manuscript evolved, two old friends, Robert Rack and Nancy Nolan took center stage. Bob, a beloved friend for over forty-five years, played an important role in every stage of my professional life. As Director of the Law Enforcement Assistance Administration (LEAA) in the 1970s, he had federal funds to disperse. We met when I sought, and his office granted, funding for expansion of my fledging public defender office. As the initiator of the practice of mediation in the U.S. Courts of Appeals, he had the experience and credibility to stand strong and support me when as CBA president I wavered about promoting a mediation center. On a more personal level, still vivid in my memory is his compassionate partnership in the exploration of the grieving process after Len's death seventeen years ago. The richness of our continued friendship is on full display in the Foreword he wrote for this book.

Some years ago, in a conversation with Bob's wife, Chris Lottman, also a dear friend, a professor of Social Work, and the kindest person I know, I mentioned some fearful thoughts I was trying to push aside. The next day she sent me these words which ever since have been taped to my desk for easy reference: "Facing your fears is a kind of doing battle—no longer running from them and acknowledging them—coming out the other side is so strengthening and ultimately worth it. Not knowing how it will turn out but facing it anyway is sometimes part of the power of the process—-which beats the hell out of the alternative." When some aspect of bringing this book to my audience has stoked anxiety, I've called upon these words or sought a conversation with Chris. My gratitude for our friendship knows no bounds.

Nancy Nolan and I met in 1987 at the Cincinnati Bar Association when I was the newly elected first woman president and she was the communications director. With sensitively she navigated office staff tensions to my great benefit, promoted my efforts and drew my lasting gratitude. Thereafter our friendship waned as life took us both in new directions. My great good fortune was to reconnect with her and quickly recognize that her expertise, my trust in her values, our prior friendship and good working relationship, was just what was needed. As a well-organized skilled editor, as my amanuensis, she set clear goals for each of us and saw to it they were met. Sometimes she pushed and I pushed back. In the end, her professional judgment usually won the day. Nancy made this book venture a reality.

A number of notable persons agreed to read my manuscript in advance of publication and offer a concise comment to entice others to do so post-publication. What a wonderful gift I received from these esteemed friends and colleagues.

Nathaniel R. Jones, one of our nation's most respected jurists, Judge of the U.S. Court of Appeals for the Sixth Circuit (1979-2002), remains active in his law firm, Blank Rome, LLC. I am proud to call him a friend and colleague of long standing. His celebrated legacy as a fighter for civil rights from his earliest years, leading to his service as General Counsel of the NAACP (1969-1979) when crucial battles were won, some lost, marked his career prior to his appointment to the bench. In 2016, his book *Answering The Call: An Autobiography of the Modern Struggle to End Racial Discrimination in America,* was published to national acclaim. It is a magnificent book. Sadly he must now watch many of the victories for which he fought be walked back. It must break his heart.

For the last fifty-four years, Jack Sherman has been my dear friend. We met when we both entered Salmon P. Chase Law School in 1965, I one of only two women in our graduating class and Jack the only black. We became law partners upon graduation and together established a public defender office in 1972. A few years later Jack left me in charge of the office and returned to our law school, this time as a professor of Constitutional Law. Both of us stood for election to the Municipal Court bench in 1979, an all white male bench at the time. We both lost. But Jack went on to have an illustrious career as a judge in both State and Federal courts. For me, he has been a beacon, a moral touchstone and some one I could always turn to for counsel and loving support.

Jack fell into the honey pot eight years ago when he became the life partner of Charlene Ventura, a woman of distinction who when young was a prominent feminist leader in Cincinnati as the second wave of the women's movement emerged. She soon went on to be the voice of those subjected to domestic violence, and as the long serving CEO of the Cincinnati YWCA fought for over forty years for both women's rights and racial equality, the mission of the organization she led. To my great good fortune, Charlene has become part of my intimate circle of friends and a supporter of my writing efforts.

If you know a psychologist, do what you can to turn them into a good friend. I have been smart enough to do just that. When I closed my office door I felt a sense of loss at no longer being able to use the competence earned over many years to guide those who no longer were safe and secure in a loving relationship. Writing about and sharing the knowledge I'd gained seemed one answer. Yet, in the face of the daily coverage of hyper-partisan political actions tearing our country apart, even friend from friend, I questioned whether writing about personal relationships at a turning point made sense. I posed this question to my psychologist friend, Dr. Susan J. Steinberg. Her response, "Nothing is more unifying than the sharing of personal stories of the human condition." This was the validation I needed. The book project would go forward. Along the way, Susan's advice was sought again and again.

It was only after Karen Faaborg retired from her high level administrative posts at the University of Cincinnati that we met and became friends, although I knew her by reputation. For some years now she is someone I consult with at every turn of events that calls for intelligent empathetic understanding. Not infrequently issues leading to the publication of this book consumed our long lunch conversations much to my great benefit. In recent years she has been facing the illness of her beloved husband (who urges her out the door to be with friends and take part in community events) much as I experienced this tender time with Len in his declining years. I treasure the time she spends with me, and the wisdom she shares.

For many of the most active years of my law practice, John Norwine served as the Executive Director of the Cincinnati Bar Asso-

ciation. As an admirer of his leadership of the Bar, I sought his counsel. And I still remember a Bar meeting when by chance I was seated
next to his wife, Perri. She told me she always turned first to my column in the monthly CBA Report. Perhaps only other writers who regularly send their words out to unknown readers know how much such
comments cheer one on. John's significant support of my career was
capped by his generous comment after reading my manuscript.

My good friend and colleague, Sherry Davis, fellow family law
practitioner and mediator, is someone I have continued to turn to for
advice over the years. When in my essays I refer to a colleague with
whom I talked over a professional problem, most often that colleague
was Sherry. Her value as a friend increased ten-fold when some years
ago she introduced me to her life-partner, Robert (Bob) Schulman, a
wise psychiatrist and now fellow author. Both individually and together they have steadfastly supported my road to publication.

It has only been in recent years that I have connected with Woody
Mosten, lawyer and national leader, author and educator in the family
law and mediation world. Woody reached out to Professor Marjorie
Aaron at the University of Cincinnati College of Law to obtain the
seven-hour teaching video she had produced of my conducting a full
series of mediation sessions (with actors playing husband and wife).
Using this as a teaching tool for his class at UCLA, he asked me to
participate in person by Skype. What an honor to be asked questions
by his graduate level students seeking to enhance their mediation
skills.

Many years ago, a close friend of mine, Dona Lansky, was scheduled for major surgery at a time when her health was already in a fragile state. Another friend, not well known to me at the time, Diane
Shank, former nurse, lawyer, and hospital risk manager, offered to
meet Dona's husband and a group of her friends to teach us how we
might advocate for her during her hospitalization. This turned a dreaded disruption of Dona's life into a successful and loving experience
for all of those who took part. Our close friendship was born. Some

years later I learned that Diane and her doctor husband, Reed, were writing a book about how patients and their families could best navigate complex health care systems. Is it any wonder that we now meet regularly to share a meal and also share what we have learned along the way to publication?

Some years ago, I took part in a lawyer-mentoring program sponsored by the Ohio Supreme Court and was paired with a young recent law school graduate, Jeanelle (Nellie) Gonzalez Mehta. A cherished friendship developed and grew far beyond the professional connection. In recent years, until her husband, Samir, was transferred to the D.C. area, we met often in my living room when her practice allowed and her youngsters were in school. We found that our separation in age by many decades was of little consequence. At times she was the advisor and I the learner. It was Nellie who one day suggested my book title: *The Third Person in the Room.*

Two other friends provided loving support to me as this book project evolved. My neighbor, Laurie Briggs, frequently comes by for serious conversations about our mutual endeavors. Two committed introverts, we waste no time on small talk and quickly get to the heart of whatever thoughts or editing tasks need to be sorted out. Jeannine Barbeau regularly appears to minister to whatever needs have been added to a list of chores beyond my ken, and offers valuable insights on the organization of my writing efforts. Both of these accomplished lawyers have taken on a daughter-like role, and they significantly enhance my day-to-day life.

Another lawyer friend, Jerry Lawson, although never specifically drawn into this book project, deserves my heartfelt thanks for having played such an important role in the development of my professional life as a mediator. In 1988, together we opened The Center for Resolution of Disputes, I as the first Board Chair and he as Director for the next eighteen years. At the outset, we attended mediation training together at the Harvard Project on Negotiation and in the years that followed, I frequently sought his counsel when stymied by a difficult case or seeking new insights. His door was always open and I drew upon his skill both as mediator and teacher to my great benefit. Although not named, he actually appears in a number of my essays. Now in retirement, he remains a treasured friend.

For the past twelve years, my articles have been published in the monthly Report of the Cincinnati Bar Association, a process facilitated by the Directors of Communications who have served over the years: Carole Branch, Julie Borths and most recently Aris Taylor. I've been served well by their friendly professionalism and positive comments.

Max Nolan contributed his graphic artist skills, significantly enhancing the book design. And thanks go to Paula Norton for her outstanding photography and adroit ability to put a reluctant subject at ease. Our recent photo shoot resulted in the photograph on the cover of the book.

I would be remiss to end these expressions of gratitude without mention of my dear brother-in-law, Len's younger brother, Curt Larsen, who I first met when he was but nine years old. In his mature years he became expert on the genealogy of the Larsen clan and so was able to provide me with historical data for this book. In 1999, he and his dear wife, Judy, hosted a still memorable family celebration on the lawn of their lovely Maryland waterside home when Len and I reached our fiftieth wedding anniversary, a well remembered joyous day.

Visit Bea Larsen on her blog at www.bealarsen.com.
I hope you enjoyed reading *The Third Person in the Room,*
and will consider reviewing it on Amazon.com.

Made in the USA
Middletown, DE
12 September 2019